IB Music Revision Guide 3rd Edition

IB Music Revision Guide
3rd Edition

Everything You Need to Prepare
for the Music Listening Examination
(Standard and Higher Level 2019–2021)

Roger Paul

ANTHEM PRESS

Anthem Press
An imprint of Wimbledon Publishing Company
www.anthempress.com

This edition first published in UK and USA 2014
by ANTHEM PRESS 75–76 Blackfriars Road, London SE1 8HA,
UK or PO Box 9779, London SW19 7ZG, UK
and
244 Madison Ave #116, New York, NY 10016, USA

British Library Cataloguing-in-Publication Data
A catalogue record for this book is available from the British Library.

ISBN-13: 978-1-78308-866-9 (Pbk)
ISBN-10: 1-78308-866-4 (Pbk)

This title is also available as an e-book.

CONTENTS

INTRODUCTION

For the Music section of the IB Diploma you have to complete the following tasks, depending on whether you are taking Higher Level (HL) or Standard Level (SL):

Higher Level – the following tasks are compulsory:

- Solo Performing (20 minutes of recordings) – 25% of the total mark
- Creating (3 pieces of work made from a combination of composing, arranging, music technology and pastiche) – 25% of the total mark
- Musical links investigation – a media script (up to 2,000 words) looking into music from two distinct cultures – 20% of the total mark
- Listening examination (2½ hours) – 30% of the total mark

Standard Level – students choose **one** of the following, which is worth 50% of the total mark:

- Solo Performing (15 minutes of recordings)
- Creating (2 pieces of work made from a combination of composing, arranging, music technology and pastiche)
- Group Performing (20–30 minutes of recordings in front of an audience)

The remaining 50% is made up of tasks common to both the HL and SL programmes:

- Musical links investigation – a media script (up to 2,000 words) looking into music from two distinct cultures – 20% of the total mark
- Listening examination (2 hours) – 30% of the total mark

As you can see, both HL and SL students produce a Musical links investigation and study for a Listening Paper. This book will help you prepare for the Listening Paper, which lasts 2½ hours for HL, 2 hours for SL. The paper is divided into 2 sections for both HL and SL. Section A is based on the Prescribed Works, Section B is based on Musical Styles and Cultures (a CD is provided).

All questions in either version of the Listening Paper are worth 20 marks. The total marks for the SL paper is 80 (20 for answering 1 question in Section A, 60 for 3 questions in Section B). The HL paper carries a total of 100 marks (40 for answering 2 questions in Section A, 60 for 3 questions in Section B). The differences between the HL and SL papers are shown in more detail below.

Higher Level:

- Section A (prescribed works) – choose **either question 1 or 2,** followed by question 3, a musical links question on the prescribed works
- Section B – choose **either question 4 or 5**, questions 6 and 7 are compulsory
- 5 questions in 2 ½ hours (150 minutes) = 30 minutes per question

Standard Level:

- Section A (prescribed works) – choose **either question 1 or 2**. The links question on the prescribed works mentioned above is **not required** for SL candidates
- Section B – choose **either question 3 or 4**, questions 5 and 6 are compulsory
- 4 questions in 2 hours (120 minutes) = 30 minutes per question

The examinations take place in May for the Northern Hemisphere and November for the Southern Hemisphere. But whenever your final term starts, try to ensure you have completed all of the coursework assignments so that you will have enough time left to revise fully for the Listening Paper.

Section A: Prescribed Works

2019:   *Brandenburg Concerto No. 2 in F major BWV1047* (c.1719–21) – J. S.
               Bach
               Dances of Galánta (1933) – Zoltán Kodály
2020–2021:   *Rhapsody on a Theme of Paganini (1934)* – Sergei Rachmaninoff
               Symphony No. 94 in G Major 'Surprise' (1791) – Joseph Haydn

Each of the first two questions focuses on musical elements found in the individual works. All candidates choose **either question 1 or 2**. Typically these questions ask you to discuss musical elements in each set work with reference to their historical context (e.g. 'demonstrate how Mozart's "Jupiter" Symphony is typical of the Classical period'). Question 3 is for HL candidates only and will require an exploration of musical links between the two prescribed works.

You may take clean scores of the prescribed works into the exam so it is worth learning how to read and navigate them as this will enable you to find points to make and give precise examples to illustrate your answers, instead of having to rely on recalling large amounts of 'crammed' information. The examiners are particularly looking for:

- Valid, relevant musical observations
- Accurately located and explained examples
- Correct use of musical terms

From page 11 onwards you will find analyses of the prescribed works and some practice questions for you to try.

Section B: Analysing Music from Different Times and Places

In this section all candidates answer 3 questions from a choice of 4. The first two are taken from Western Classical music, while the other two feature extracts from Jazz, Pop and World music. Candidates are allowed to choose between the Western Classical questions. Western Classical in IB is 'classical' in the record shop sense, in that the questions are drawn from the Renaissance period up to the present-day 'Modern' period. The titles and composers of the extracts are also usually given in the question headings.

Section B questions always ask you to 'analyse, examine and discuss in detail what you hear (or see in a given score) in this extract'. These are open-ended questions but the examiners are looking to award marks for:

- Describing musical elements (instruments/voices, tempo, duration, melody, harmony, tonality, texture)
- Using the correct terminology when describing the musical elements
- Outlining the structure of the music
- Outlining the context of the music (period, date, composer, genre, purpose)

A score is usually provided for one of these questions and you are expected to refer to it in your answer. The accompanying CD tracks can be played as often as you wish (including during the 5 minutes' reading time at the start), and your school/college should provide a CD player capable of displaying minutes and seconds. This is important because it is the only way of giving precise locations for your examples when no score is provided. Notice that Section B carries more marks than Section A. You should practise this type of question as frequently as you can, given that music extracts are so accessible nowadays. Although musical styles have distinguishing features, it is dangerous to assume that only those features will be heard. *You must write about what you actually hear, not just what you expect to hear.* Please see page 79 for an overview of the main styles and some practice questions; suggested answers for these are on page 121.

Continuous Prose or Note Form? Watch the Time ...

The IB guide states that in all questions you are required to 'build a case'. While there is no requirement to write in continuous prose, the use of bullet points is not without risk. There is a danger that bullet points could be too brief and could lose you marks because you have not expressed the point in enough detail. Conversely some candidates get bogged down writing what to them feels like an essay, and you must also be mindful of the time. Remember you have around 30 minutes per question. How much of this is writing time? Remember that some of your time will be used up on thinking, planning, looking at scores and, in the case of Section B, listening to CD extracts. Although these extracts tend to be around 1'30"–2'00" in length you will need to play them more than once. You must work quickly and efficiently in this exam, so I usually advise my students to:

- Briefly plan the answer – you must arrange your ideas into a logical argument, and you may still get some credit even if you run out of time.
- Write in what I call 'detailed bullet points'. Make the point, give the precise location of your example and explain it.
- Leave gaps between your points so that they can be developed later if you suddenly think of something else you could mention that is related. This will help you to keep your answer organised.

MUSICAL TERMS AND DEVICES

This section of the guide is an introduction to the technical terms used in the IB music course. They are listed under the 'elements' of music (i.e. structure, melody, rhythm, tonality, harmony, texture, forces and context) they relate to, so that in the examination you will be able to give relevant answers to whatever question is set. You would not score many marks – and waste a lot of time – if you wrote, for example, about polyphonic texture in a question asking you to comment on the use of melody.

Read these terms carefully and note which elements they are associated with. Notice that some terms can be used under more than one element, e.g. 'pedal point' is both a harmonic and a textural device. Refer to the Glossary at the back of the book if you are unfamiliar with any of them, and practise identifying them with both your eyes and ears, in scores and recordings.

Tip: use the word '**mostly**' to help clarify your answers. For example, melodies often have both steps and leaps, but if there are more steps, this could be described more accurately as 'mostly conjunct'.

Structure	• Binary (AB, AABB) • Ternary (ABA) • Rondo (ABACA, etc.) • Theme and variations (A1A2A3A4, etc.), variations on a Ground Bass • Sonata form (exposition/development/recapitulation) • Ritornello • Fugue • Songs: Strophic (same music for each verse), through-composed (ABCD etc.), verse/bridge/chorus/middle eight/instrumental solo, 32-bar song (AABA) • 12-bar blues (AAB) • Jazz: head arrangement (theme, improvised solos, theme) • Raga: alap/jor/gat/jhalla

Melody	• Conjunct (stepwise) movement
	• Disjunct (angular) movement
	• Range of the melody (narrow/wide, interval between highest/lowest notes)
	• Key/scale of the melody: major/minor, modal, atonal, blues, raga, slendro, etc.
	• Use of chromatic notes/accidentals
	• Important motifs, used to build themes
	• Ornaments: passing notes, auxiliary notes, appoggiaturas, grace notes, trills, mordents, turns, etc.
	• Phrasing: regular/irregular, question and answer, long/short
	• Flowing or fragmented
	• Repetition, rising/falling sequence
	• Vocal melodies: word-setting (syllabic/melismatic), word-painting
Rhythm	• Time signature or metre: simple, e.g. 2, 3, 4 beats in a bar; compound, e.g. 5 or more beats in a bar
	• Changes of time signature or metre
	• The range of different note lengths used
	• Important rhythmic motifs or patterns in a piece
	• Dotted rhythms
	• Triplets and other unusual groupings
	• Syncopated or offbeat rhythms
	• Cross rhythms, e.g. Hemiola
	• Polyrhythms
	• Accents
	• Ostinato patterns
	• Swing or shuffle rhythm, e.g. in Jazz or Blues
	• Flexible, *ad lib* patterns with no fixed metre
Tonality	• Tonal: major or minor key
	• Functional harmony, i.e. the key is defined by clear cadences
	• Non-functional harmony, i.e. few/no cadences, but still uses the notes of the key
	• Atonal (no key)
	• Modal, e.g. pentatonic, Aeolian, Dorian, Phrygian, etc.
	• Modulations (changes of tonality/key) in the music

Harmony	• Triads (major/minor/diminished/augmented), root position or inverted • Diatonic (uses the notes of the key) • Chromatic (with accidentals) • Functional harmony, i.e. the key is defined by clear cadences • Non-functional harmony, i.e. few/no cadences, but still uses the notes of the key • Cadences (perfect/imperfect/plagal/interrupted) • Pedals (tonic/dominant, in the bass/inverted) • Circle of 5ths • Tierce de Picardie (minor piece ends on a tonic major chord) • 7th chords (dominant/major/minor/diminished) • Extended chords: 9th, 11th, 13th • Augmented 6th, diminished 7th, Neapolitan 6th • Dissonances: false relation, suspension, appoggiatura
Texture	• Monophonic (one solo line) • Homophonic (chordal, melody and chords) • Arpeggios (broken chords), Alberti Bass • Polyphonic (2 or more independent lines) • Fugal • Detached (staccato) or sustained (legato) chords • Parts in unison or octaves • The number of parts in the music (2, 3, 4, etc.) • Parallel motion, e.g. 3rds/6ths • Contrary motion • Pedals (tonic/dominant, in the bass/inverted) • Imitation • Canon (exact imitation) • Antiphony (Call and Response in some cultures) • Ostinato (Riff in popular music/jazz)
Forces	The voices/instruments/sounds used in the music: • Tessitura (register or range) • Glissando, falls, pitch bends • Strings: bowed, plucked, harmonics, muted • Piano: sustain/soft pedals • Guitars: acoustic/electric, rhythm/lead, clean/distorted
Context	The purpose or occasion for which the music was created: • Religious ceremony or ritual • Public entertainment, e.g. concert, theatre • Mass media, e.g. studio recording, film and television • Dancing or celebration • Private entertainment, e.g. for a patron (royalty, aristocracy), for family/friends to perform themselves

Section A

PRESCRIBED WORKS 2019

BRANDENBURG CONCERTO NO. 2 IN F MAJOR BWV1047 (c.1719–21)
J. S. BACH

Introduction

This Prescribed Work is the second of a set of 6 concertos scored for a variety of instrumental combinations which Johann Sebastian Bach sent to Christian-Ludwig, Margrave of Brandenburg-Schwedt in 1721. Concerto No. 2 is believed to have been composed in or around 1719. The Margrave had asked Bach to send him some of his compositions and it is most likely all 6 concertos were written during the period Bach was employed as *Kapellmeister* to the Prince of Anhalt-Köthen. Indeed most of Bach's chamber and orchestral music dates from his time in this post.

These concertos are mostly of a type called Concerto Grosso (literally '*big concert*'), a popular genre among middle to late Baroque composers including Corelli, Vivaldi, Handel and of course Bach. A Concerto Grosso features two contrasting instrumental groups: the **concertino**, a smaller group of soloists, and the **ripieno**, the tutti or full orchestra (usually strings). Both of these groups were accompanied by the **continuo**, which is heard in almost all Baroque music, most commonly a harpsichord and cello, which provided the harmonic filling and bass line respectively. While both groups would have shared some of the same musical material, other themes were played exclusively by the concertino. Furthermore, the part writing for the concertino group was usually more virtuosic and elaborate.

Bach was known as an experimenter, as can be seen in this work, with its unusual concertino group of tromba, (treble) recorder, oboe and violin; his often novel approach to musical structures; and his daring use of harmony and dissonance.

Instrumentation

The 'tromba' referred to by Bach in his score was a natural trumpet in high F, with no valves which meant it played only the notes of the harmonic series.

The sound of the tromba in the 18th century was softer in both timbre and dynamic compared to a modern trumpet, which explains why Bach was able to use it in a concertino group alongside a treble recorder, oboe and violin without any problems with balance. The solo tromba part Bach wrote was at one time regarded as unplayable, because of technical difficulties and tuning issues on certain harmonics. It is highly likely he had a particular performer in mind for this part, since virtuoso trumpet and horn players would travel around Europe and were highly sought after. But with research into Baroque performance techniques and construction leading to the development of the so-called Baroque Trumpet, these problems have been overcome and many fine recordings of this work have been made since.

Bach's score also calls for a 'violone' in the ripieno strings. The violone was a name given to a variety of lower stringed instruments, but it is most likely he intended the part to be played by one of the larger double bass viols, similar in size to the modern double bass. Like the double bass the violone sounds an octave lower than written; therefore, it adds real depth to the sound of the orchestra.

1st Movement

Context	A lively opening movement in the Concerto Grosso style. Although Bach gave a 2/2 time signature there is no tempo indication; the movement is usually played at a moderate tempo with a 4/4 crotchet pulse.
Themes and Motifs	The 8-bar main tutti Ritornello theme is built from four 2-bar motifs, each starting with an **anacrusis** on the upbeat: 1. 1st tutti motif b1 (see below) – outlining a tonic F major triad with B♭ passing notes, with a rising **dactylic** ♪ ♪♪ rhythm. Repeated in b2. 2. 2nd tutti motif bb3-4 – consists of mostly conjunct semiquavers. 3. 3rd tutti motif bb5-6 – derived from the 1st motif, once again outlining the tonic triad with passing notes, but now with a falling dactylic pattern. 4. 4th tutti motif bb7-8 – similar to the 2nd in rhythm. Mostly semiquavers outlining the tonic and dominant 7th chords, before a cadence in the tonic decorated with a trill. 5. An additional tutti motif (bb1-2) can also be heard in the bass parts as a counterpoint to the 1st motif; it revolves conjunctly around the tonic F mostly in semiquavers.

	There are also two additional concertino themes (again both anacrusic) used exclusively by the soloists: 6. bb9-10 – *1st concertino theme*, heard in the violin to begin with, rises in steps to the tonic with a trill on the leading note E before dropping an octave and becoming more arpeggic in nature. 7. bb32-35 – *2nd concertino theme*, a quaver motif played in imitation, initially between the tromba and the oboe. It is taken from the C-F-C quavers in the 1st tutti motif (b1$^{3-4}$ upper parts).
Structure and Tonality	118 bars, F major, in **ritornello form** with the main *tutti* motifs returning in different combinations in a variety of related keys between *episodes* for the four soloists, who have their own additional exclusive themes. • bb1-8 – opening tutti in F major • bb9-22 – 1st episode, modulates to the dominant (C major). Each soloist presents the 1st concertino theme, with 2-bar tutti interjections in between • bb23-28 – shortened 2nd tutti in C major (6 bars) • bb29-35 – 2nd episode in F major, moving towards D minor. Tromba reprises 1st concertino theme, and then presents the 2nd in imitation with the oboe • bb36-39 – 3rd tutti in D minor (4 bars) • bb40-55 – 3rd episode, developing the tutti motifs, starting from D minor and moving through two harmonic sequences (circle of 5ths followed by a 3 × 2-bar sequence of dominant 7ths towards B♭ major • bb56-59 – 4th tutti in B♭ major (4 bars), with the opening motif in the bass for 2 bars • bb60-67 – 4th episode featuring the 1st concertino theme, moving towards C minor • bb68-71 – 5th tutti in C minor • bb72-79 – 5th episode, featuring the 2nd concertino theme b76, moving towards G minor • bb80-83 – 6th tutti in G minor • bb84-102 – 6th episode, moving through D minor and A minor. Further thematic development (e.g. 1st tutti motif in double canon soli b94) • bb103-118 – final tutti in F major, with a restatement of all the tutti motifs, briefly interrupted by the 3 × 2-bar sequence of dominant 7ths heard earlier (b107)
Melodic Development	Bach is highly creative with the many ways in which he juggles his motifs: • Motifs in **counterpoint**, e.g. 1st and 5th tutti motifs, b1 upper parts and bass. This 5th bass motif is later heard in the tromba above the 1st (b19).

	• 2nd concertino theme b32³ is accompanied by the ripieno bass playing part of the 2nd tutti motif in a circle of 5ths sequence. • 5th tutti motif in **contrary motion** (recorder/oboe/violin) as the tromba plays the 1st (b40). • Bach '**spins out**' (German = *fortspinnung*) the 3rd tutti motif between the soloists, above a chromatic harmonic sequence of dominant 7th chords, leading to the same motif appearing in the ripieno bass in B♭ major (bb50-57). • **Extra notes** added to the 1st tutti motif (D, bb86-87 solo violin). • 1st tutti motif in **canon** (bb87-88 ripieno bass leading off, followed by tromba 2 beats after). This is followed up later by a double canon for the soloists (b93⁴ recorder/violin in 6ths, tromba/oboe in 3rds 2 beats after).

Harmony	• bb1-8 – entirely **diatonic**, mostly primary triads in root position and 1st inversion, with a Ic-V-I perfect cadence b8.
	  o **Dissonance** results from passing notes and auxiliary notes (b3 recorder/oboe/violin)
	  o Accented passing notes decorating the cadence mentioned above (b8 B♭ over the F major chord resolving to the A, recorder/oboe/violin)
	• Continuo bass part also decorated with passing notes, e.g. b9² (A) and b9⁴ (G).
	• Modulations to related keys confirmed by perfect cadences, e.g. dominant C major b28, relative minor (D) b39.
	• bb32-36 – complete **circle of 5ths** starting and ending on D minor chord. This is most clearly seen in the violone part.
	• There are also some **chromatic** chords and progressions:
	  o 2-bar sequence of dominant 7ths:

	    F⁷/E♭ D⁷ G⁷/F E⁷
	  o b112 – diminished 7th chord on B♮
	• b64 recorder – chain of 9-8 **suspensions**

Texture	A wide variety of textures abound in this movement, polyphonic in the main supported by the ripieno and continuo parts filling in the harmony. • bb1-2 – two of the ritornello motifs are heard in **counterpoint** together in the upper parts and the cello/violone • bb9-22 – contrast in textures between solo passages with continuo and alternating tutti interjections • bb32³-35 – 2nd concertino theme heard in antiphonal **imitation** (tromba and oboe) with the following accompaniments: o **double-stopped** solo violin

	o counterpoint from the ritornello bass theme first heard in bb1-2 played in parallel 3rds (recorder and continuo) o ripieno violins play sustained notes to fill in the harmony and bind the other independent lines together • bb50-55 – a more homophonic accompaniment can be heard underneath the soloists' polyphony: o detached chords, ripieno strings o repeated cello/violone bass notes o ripieno 1st violin outlines the harmony in syncopated crotchets • bb70-71 – **antiphonal** octave G's between upper and lower ripieno strings/continuo • b87⁴ – **canon** between violone/continuo and tromba half a bar later • b93⁴ – double canon between recorder/violin and tromba/oboe, each pair moving in **parallel motion** • b102⁴ – 1st ritornello motif heard in **unison** across all parts including the continuo harpsichord ('**tasto solo**' = play the notes with no chords)
Rhythm	• The time signature is 'cut time' which usually means 2 minims in a bar. However Bach does not give a tempo marking and most performances given today have a moderate 4 in a bar pulse. • The continuo cello and violone parts move mostly in quavers and semiquavers which drives the music onwards with purpose. • The 1st and 3rd ritornello motifs both feature dactylic rhythmic patterns (i.e. long-short-short). • All of the thematic material is anacrusic, starting with an upbeat. • Syncopated crotchet accompaniment (bb50-55 ripieno 1st violin).

2nd Movement: Andante

Context	A calm and expressive Andante in the relative minor to contrast with the more vigorous outer movements. The tromba and ripieno strings do not play here, leaving a more intimate chamber-like ensemble of recorder, oboe, violin and continuo.
Structure and Tonality	65 bars, a fugal discussion of two simple melodic ideas. Although the continuo never plays either of these melodies and remains in its role as the accompanist, the three solo parts bear many of the hallmarks of a fugue as outlined below: • bb1-7 – Exposition, D minor. The violin announces the fugue **subject**, followed immediately by real answers in the tonic from the oboe and recorder. During these answers the **countersubject** is introduced (violin bb3³-5¹, oboe bb5³-7¹). • bb8-23 – Episode, during which the key moves through A minor and cadences in C major. The subject is developed in a series of new variants.

	• bb23³-33 – Middle Entries, in C major and modulating to B♭ major. The subject is varied again in the violin and recorder, but the oboe restates the original in a brief return to the tonic (b27³). • bb33-37 – brief episode where the countersubject is varied and passed around the soloists in a **circle of 5ths**. • bb37³-43 – Middle entries in G minor. • bb43³-57 – Episode, starting with the oboe playing a subject variant from b7³ in the tonic, before an extended discussion of the countersubject across a complete circle of 5ths ending on V of D minor. • bb57³-65 – Final entries in the tonic first in the violin, followed by the oboe. The last recorder entry is an extended cadential version of the subject, ending on a **Tierce de Picardie** b65.
Melodic Development	Bach skilfully makes the most of his two simple melodic ideas: **Subject**  • Mostly conjunct, narrow range of a minor 6th, anacrusic, diatonic, **anapaestic** rhythmic figure (b2³), decorated at the end with a trill and an accented passing note (E, b3²). **Countersubject**  • Also mostly conjunct and anacrusic. Two short falling figures which are either a suspension or an appoggiatura; the second is a decorated descending sequence of the first. • The opening F-F-E figure was originally heard in the 1st movement (bb63⁴-65, recorder) and could be thought of as a motif which unifies the concerto as a whole. • Notice how the use of crotchet rests contrasts with the Subject and creates holes in the texture so that each part can be heard more clearly. Several variants of both the subject and the countersubject can be heard as the movement progresses. **Subject** • b7³ recorder – now in A minor, the first quaver is replaced by two semiquavers. Also note the expressive falling diminished 4th C-G# b8³. Heard again in the tonic later (b43³ oboe). • b9³ oboe – the first interval in the anapaestic figure is widened to a perfect 5th, and the crotchet from b3¹ is replaced by two quavers forming an additional accented passing note in a descending scale.

<table>
<tr><td></td><td>

- b13³ recorder – a shorter cadential variant ending more decisively as a crotchet on the first beat of the bar.
- b23³ violin – the rhythm of b3 has been elaborated with two dactylic patterns. Imitated by the recorder two bars later.
- b61³ recorder – extended to a 4-bar phrase by repeating the anapaestic figure before cadencing on the tonic, decorated with an anticipation b64³.

Countersubject

- b7¹ violin – instead of falling, the appoggiatura rises to the tonic
- b19³ oboe/violin – played in parallel 3rds
- b33² oboe – starts one beat earlier with an additional crotchet. This variant is passed around the soloists in a circle of 5ths sequence with parallel 3rds and 6ths
- b50³ – a series of sequential double suspensions passed between the soloists in pairs

The continuo cello line maintains a harmonic outline in quavers, stopping only for important cadences.
</td></tr>
</table>

Harmony	<ul><li>largely diatonic, with modulations confirmed by cadences, e.g. Ic-V-I in A minor bb14-15.</li><li>however, cadence points like this also contain dissonance resulting from the polyphonic lines of the soloists:<ul><li>parallel 9ths (b14 oboe and continuo cello)</li><li>the violin C at the end of b14 clashes with the E major chord played by the continuo harpsichord</li><li>the A minor chord on the next beat (b15¹) has two accented passing notes running through it (oboe and violin in 3rds) before briefly resolving onto harmony notes</li></ul></li><li>Circle of 5ths sequence – a complete circle can be traced, starting and ending on A (bb49-56 cello).</li><li>Interrupted cadence V-VI in D minor bb62-63 helps to extend the final phrase by delaying the expected perfect cadence.</li><li>Hemiola bb63-64 reinforced by two striking diminished 7th chords on B♭ and B♮, before resolving to the final Ic-V-I cadence in D minor.</li><li>Tierce de Picardie on the final tonic chord b65</li></ul>
Rhythm	<ul><li>3/4 time throughout, Andante</li><li>Almost continuous cello quavers push the movement along, with cadences marked by crotchets</li><li>Anapaestic rhythm ♪♪♩ in the fugue subject (b2³)</li><li>The subject and countersubject both start with an anacrusis</li><li>**Hemiola** bb63-64, most clearly seen in the cello part</li></ul>

Texture	• Fugal texture for the soloists, with harmonic support from the continuo cello and harpsichord
	• Canonic imitation of the fugue subject (bb1-7 soloists)
	• Parallel motion (b12 oboe and violin in 3rds)
	• Contrary motion (bb50-54 soloists' imitation of the countersubject in pairs)

3rd Movement: Allegro Assai

Context	This movement resembles the 1st movement in many ways; vigorous energy, and similar thematic and rhythmic material cast in a ritornello form in F major. However, the ripieno strings' role is very much reduced, given that they are silent for the first 46 bars, and when they do play it is more as an accompaniment to the soloists than was the case in the opening movement.

Structure and Tonality	139 bars, which can be thought of as a ritornello form with some fugal elements as explained below.
	Fugue – bb1-46 for the 4 soloists accompanied by the continuo
	
	• Exposition bb1-33
	  o b1 – Subject (F major) announced by the tromba which was silent for the 2nd movement. There is also an imitative 1st countersubject (CS1) announced at the same time by the continuo. These two themes are always heard together throughout.
	  o b7 – Real Answer in the oboe, CS1 still in the continuo. Another countersubject (CS2) is played by the tromba.
	  o b13 – a shorter third countersubject (CS3) is introduced by the oboe and imitated by the tromba 2 bars later.
	  o b21 – Subject in the violin.
	  o b27 – Answer in the recorder.
	  o b33 – a fugal Episode for recorder, oboe, violin plus continuo
	• Middle entry
	  o b41 – Subject (C major) restated by the tromba. The continuo falls silent in order to lend weight to the entry of the ripieno.
	
	Ritornello – b47 onwards, the movement changes into a more typical concerto grosso format with alternate tutti and solo episode sections (interestingly these ritornello episodes are based on the subject and countersubjects from the opening fugue, which gives the impression that they could be fugal Middle Entries!).
	
	• b47 – Tutti, C major. A new tutti theme, derived from the fugue subject, is announced by the oboe, closely imitated by the tromba and violin.
	• b53 – Episode (C major moving to D minor). Subject played by the violin, answered by the oboe.

	• b72 – Tutti, D minor. The Subject is now heard in the ripieno violone and continuo, which then move into a restatement of the Tutti theme imitated by the tromba and recorder. • b85 – Episode, in which the soloists each present CS3 first heard in b13. Starting in D minor, each entry moves sequentially around the circle of 5ths towards B♭ major. • b97 – Tutti, B♭ major. Featuring the Tutti theme in the tromba, closely imitated by the oboe, violone and continuo. The other accompanying parts enter in a stretto. • b107 – Episode, B♭ major. The Subject is played by the oboe and answered by the recorder (b113) as the music moves back towards the tonic. • b119 – Tutti, F major. Similar to that starting a b72, the Subject is heard in the violone and continuo on the dominant of F major. This leads into the Tutti theme in recorder/oboe/violin. The Subject is heard one last time in the tromba (b136) over a tonic pedal to bring the work to a close.
Melodic Development	Much of the thematic material is derived from the opening fugue Subject, which in turn can be traced back to the main Ritornello theme from the 1st movement. This gives the 3rd movement, indeed the whole concerto, a sense of thematic unity. **Subject** bb 1-4:  Similarities to the 1st movement Ritornello theme: • repeated dactylic rhythms mostly in conjunct movement • diatonic, based around the notes of the tonic triad (F, A and especially C) • a direct quotation from the opening 5 notes of the 1st movement is present in this Subject (in brackets above) • decorated by trills The Subject also contains **two motifs** which Bach uses to build more themes later on in the movement: • the opening 3 quavers (F-C-C), leaping up a perfect 5th with a pair of repeated notes • the lower auxiliary note figure (C-B♭-C) in b1² Examples: 2nd countersubject (CS2, b7 tromba)  • Starts with the 3 quavers but varies the repeated notes with an octave leap.

3rd countersubject (CS3, bb13-14 oboe)

- Starts with the octave leap from CS2, but now tied over the barline as a suspension which resolves into the auxiliary note figure.

Tutti theme (b47 oboe)

- this theme is syncopated, starting on the 2nd quaver of b47
- the upward leap is now a perfect 4th, and there is an extra repeated quaver
- the auxiliary note figure is now inverted (b48 G-A-G)
- the two motifs then combine in a descending sequence
- the imitation starting on the last quaver of b47 (violin) alternates lower and upper auxiliary notes as a contrast to the oboe lead

Notice how the themes dissipate into semiquaver passage work to provide continuity into the next thematic statement, e.g. oboe bb7-16 plays the Subject, then semiquaver figures into CS3 followed by more semiquaver figures.

Harmony	• Mostly diatonic with modulations to related keys confirmed by perfect cadences, e.g. V-I in dominant C major bb40-41, subdominant B♭ major bb106-107. • Imperfect cadences are used to keep the music moving by avoiding the finality of a perfect cadence, e.g. I-V in C major bb62-63, and again in D minor two bars later. • b136 – tonic pedal F reinforces the tonality at the end, resulting in an unusual plagal IVc-I final cadence bb138-139.
Rhythm	• 2/4 time, Allegro assai (very fast) • The continuo cello and violone parts move mostly in quavers and semiquavers which drives the music onwards with purpose • The fugue subject features dactylic rhythmic patterns (i.e. long-short-short) • Syncopated crotchets (bb10-11 CS2, tromba) • Semiquaver passage work (e.g. bb93-105 solo violin)
Texture	• bb1-27 – fugal texture to begin with as each of the 4 soloists enters with the subject. • Ripieno strings are silent for the first 46 bars. The continuo drops out at b41 to add weight to the ripieno entry in b47. • Contrasting alternate full tutti and reduced soli/continuo textures from b47 onwards, e.g. tutti b47, soli/continuo b57, tutti b72, etc. typical of ritornello form.

- bb72-78 – contains a variety of different textures:
  - **counterpoint** between violone/continuo, recorder and ripieno 1st violin
  - detached chords tromba, ripieno 2nd violin/viola
  - **inner dominant pedal** in tromba, sounding an A in the key of D minor
- bb97-103 – tutti passage starts with **stretto** entries for all parts:
  - sustained ripieno violins
  - close imitation, one quaver apart (tromba lead, followed by oboe, violone and continuo)
  - parallel motion: recorder/violin in 6ths, oboe and violone/continuo in compound 3rds
- bb136-139 – Final Subject/CS1 entry accompanied by homophonic detached chords.

Sample Questions

In Section A of the examination there will be one question on each of the two prescribed works. You must choose to answer **one** of these **two** questions (as well as a third 'musical links' question which will be discussed later). Here are four sample questions based on the *Brandenburg Concerto No. 2* to use for practice. You may answer these in continuous prose or detailed bullet points and you should allow around 30 minutes under timed conditions to complete each question. Reference should be made to an unmarked copy of the score and remember to give precise locations for the musical features you discuss.

1. *Brandenburg Concerto No. 2* is regarded as an example of how Bach's music represents the height of the Baroque style. Discuss **at least three** contrasting passages which illustrate this view.
2. Bach uses a wide range of instrumental timbres and textures in *Brandenburg Concerto No. 2*. Discuss and illustrate this view, making detailed references to the score.
3. Discuss Bach's use of structure and tonality in the **1st movement** of *Brandenburg Concerto No. 2*.
4. Discuss the changing relationship between the soloists' and ripieno parts across each of the three movements of *Brandenburg Concerto No. 2*. Refer in detail to specific passages of music.

DANCES OF GALÁNTA (1933)
ZOLTÁN KODÁLY

Introduction

This Prescribed Work was composed by Zoltán Kodály (1882–1967) for the 80th anniversary of the Budapest Philharmonic Society in his native Hungary. He took his inspiration from the small town of Galánta, which was part of the Kingdom of Hungary during his childhood there, but is now in present-day Slovakia. Kodály explained that his inspiration for the piece came in two parts:

> At that time there existed a famous gypsy band that has since disappeared. This was the first 'orchestral' sonority that came to the ears of the child. The forebears of these gypsies were already known more than a hundred years ago. About 1800 some books of Hungarian dances were published in Vienna, one of which contained music 'after several Gypsies from Galánta'. They have preserved the old traditions. In order to keep it alive, the composer has taken his principal themes from these old publications.

Kodály chose several of these dances for his piece, with five of them making up the principal sections of the one-movement structure. He also wanted to recreate the *Verbunkos* style of the aforementioned gypsy band. *Verbunkos* was a Hungarian/Gypsy dance style with march-like accompaniments from the 18th century which was used to recruit young men into the army, with contrasting slow and fast sections, alternating swagger with foot-stomping energy and excitement.

Kodály's piece is much more than an arrangement of Gypsy folk tunes; they are infused and combined with an eclectic range of styles from 19th-century Romanticism to Impressionism and even Atonality to showcase these traditional melodies within a modern 20th-century Hungarian style of music.

Instrumentation

The piece is scored for orchestra, but not of the size often called for by 20th-century composers:

- Woodwind – 2 each of flute (2nd player also plays piccolo), oboe, clarinet, bassoon
- Brass – 4 French horns, 2 trumpets
- Percussion – timpani, triangle, campanelle (glockenspiel), tamburo piccolo (side drum)
- Strings (1st/2nd violins, violas, cellos, double basses)

Kodály gives the clarinet a prominent solo role, representing the *tárogató*, a single-reed instrument resembling a clarinet which he probably first heard in the Galánta gypsy band. The cello section is also regularly given the melody, possibly because Kodály learned to play the cello in Galánta. As an ethno-musicologist and composer, Kodály was passionate about collecting local folk tunes and creating art music that was distinctively Hungarian. His colourful orchestrations sound similar to those of the Russian nationalist composers Rimsky-Korsakov and Mussorgsky, who were also working towards a similar goal for their own country.

Structure	**N.B.** – the Universal Edition score printed bar numbers are incorrect after bar 95; there is an extra uncounted bar between b95 and b100! This is simple enough to correct, but be aware that the numberings below are based on those in the score as it stands.
	One movement with 607 bars in total. There are five principal gypsy dances (as well as some additional ones) featured in this piece. Broadly speaking, the piece follows the form of a *verbunkos*, a traditional Hungarian style of dance and instrumental music comprising two sections: slow (*lassu*) with dotted rhythms, and fast (*friss*) with wild virtuosic running semiquaver passages.
	bb1-235 – slow (*lassu*) bb236-607 – fast (*friss*)
	However, within these broad sections lies a freer, more complex structure made up of sections and subsections, with recurring themes to unify the work as a whole:
	Introduction bb1-49 – a fantasia-like opening section
	- Featuring the first of the folk melodies in this piece, and a series of 32nd note (demisemiquaver) flourishes. These 2 ideas alternate initially, and are then combined from b19. - The first melody is heard on various solo instruments, e.g. b1 cello section, b10 horn, b37 clarinet. - Clarinet cadenza b45 segues straight into....

Ritornello section bb50-235 – featuring 3 of the principal Hungarian gypsy dance melodies; the **1st Dance** acts like a recurring ritornello theme, with the **2nd** and **3rd Dances** heard as episodes.

- bb50-93 – the passionate **1st Dance** is heard in the clarinet b50, then *ff* upper strings/woodwind b66 and cellos (with a shorter version) b82. Orchestral climax at b88 starts a link passage into the next section.
- bb93-150 – **2nd Dance**, in binary form (AABB):
  - o A – a jauntier theme played by the flute b96, repeated with additional piccolo b103
  - o B – more forceful answering phrase is heard at b109 (1st violin/viola/clarinet), repeated by solo flute b113
  - o Short link passage b145 extending the B phrase
- bb151-172 – a shorter reprise of the **1st Dance** in *ff* upper strings/woodwind. Link passage from b167.
- bb173-228 – **3rd Dance**, again in binary form:
  - o A – 2 × 8-bar phrases bb173-188, solo oboe, then flute
  - o B – 2 more 8-bar phrases bb189-204, solo oboe, then piccolo
  - o Link passage where Kodály develops fragments of the B phrase, accelerating towards the next section
- bb229-235 – a brief reprise of the **1st Dance**, followed by a descending linking phrase for lower strings/woodwind

4th Dance bb236-333

- Featuring two phrases in the *friss* style; an exciting syncopated melody b236, and another with rapid semiquaver passages b268.
- Syncopated melody accelerates to a climax b334 leading straight into the next section.

Poco meno mosso bb334-420 – not quite as fast as the 4th Dance:

- 12-bar introduction establishing both the accompaniment and B♭ major tonality
- bb346-377 – another binary form folk tune similar in character to that heard earlier from b96
- bb378-420 – a link passage developing the theme and introducing hints of the next

5th Dance bb421-607 – an even faster Finale section recalling several dances from earlier in the piece:

- b421 – a short ostinato-like phrase, viola and 2nd violin in canon
- b443 – a phrase built from a 2-bar motif with a distinctive ♪♪ ♪ syncopated rhythm and semiquaver runs
- b490 – a reprise of the **4th Dance** phrases (b236 and b268). As before the syncopated melody is used to build a climax bb525-542
- b543 – **5th Dance** returns, building to a sudden pause and silence at b565

	• b566 – **Coda**: **1st Dance** ritornello reappears in its original *Andante* tempo, passing from flute to oboe and clarinet, which plays another cadenza – a reminder of the **Introduction** • b579 – a final frantic reprise of the **5th Dance**

Melody	Kodály took all of his thematic material from Gypsy dances specifically from Galánta, found in collections of Hungarian dances published in Vienna c.1800.
	
	Introduction theme bb1-5
	
	• Verbunkos style slow double-dotted rhythms with conjunct 32nd note auxiliary and passing note flourishes.
	• Dorian mode on A (ABCDEF#G); the opening F# makes the tonality uncertain to begin with.
	• Irregular 5-bar phrase.
	• Narrow range of a minor 7th typical of folk melodies.
	• Developments:
	  o b10 – transposed a 5th higher
	  o b19 – extended to 7 bars via a descending sequence
	  o bb22²-23¹ – augmented 2nd C#-B♭ typical of the verbunkos style
	  o b37 – clarinet plays a chromatic variant which rises in sequence to a climax on high C (b43)
	
	1st Dance bb50-65
	
	• Kodály replaces the original straight semiquaver rhythms with a more elaborate verbunkos-style dotted pattern with the semiquavers compressed into triplet turn-like figures:
	
	Original

	Kodály

	• Starts in E minor, ends in A minor
	• 16 bars, 2 × 8-bar mostly conjunct phrases in binary form:
	  o 1st phrase is built from a 2-bar melody repeated in a descending sequence. Usually preceded by a rising glissando up to the first note. Cadences on repeated dominant B's with a prominent rising octave leap.
	  o 2nd phrase has more quaver movement, especially the four *sostenuto* notes in b59.
	• Several Lombardic/Scotch Snap rhythms, often accenting the 3rd beat, e.g. b50³, 51³

- Developments:
  - b67 – theme is reharmonised and has a more chromatic ending bb78-79
  - b164 – the quavers of b79 are elaborated with repeated semiquavers
  - b229 – theme is heard in the Lydian Dominant scale on B♭ (B♭CDEFGA♭); the C#'s are chromatic auxiliary notes

2nd Dance bb96-118 – A♭ minor (originally in A minor), 2 phrases in AABB in binary form, ends in D♭ major.

- 1st phrase: Kodály transposed the original melody down a semitone, and again converts straight semiquavers into dotted patterns (here the dots are often replaced by 32nd note rests). Irregular phrasing; 7 bars first time, 6 bars on repeat.
- 2nd phrase: largely unchanged except for an extension to the D♭ major ending using repeated broken triads. Another verbunkos-style augmented 2nd b111 (G♮-F♭)
- Developments:
  - b123 – 1st phrase is heard in exotic sounding parallel 4ths
  - b134 – a 3-part triadic version of the 2nd phrase
  - b142 – the final D♭ broken triads now in 32nd notes and used in the following link passage

3rd Dance bb173-204 – D major, repeated 8-bar phrases in binary form (AABB), 32 bars in total.

- Both phrases share a repeated 2-bar melody with a syncopated motif at the start followed by conjunct semiquavers and quavers.
- 1st phrase: diatonic, built from a, ends on the dominant (A)
- 2nd phrase: mostly diatonic apart from one chromatic lower auxiliary note (G# b192)
- Developments:
  - The first half of the 2nd phrase is transposed into G major b205 and the more distant E♭ major b213.
  - Between these transpositions the second half of the 2nd phrase is abruptly pulled back into D major in a quicker *Animato* tempo. These sudden tempo changes are another feature of Gypsy music, and were also used by Brahms in his *Hungarian Dances*.
  - bb220-228 – the ♪♪♪♪ ♩rhythm from b204 is developed into imitative scalic figures.

4th Dance bb236-275 – 2 contrasting *Allegro* phrases:

- 1st phrase bb236-247: 2 × 6-bar phrases in A minor, each featuring a chain of conjunct syncopated crotchets with a final semiquaver flourish in the 6th bar. One phrase ends on the dominant E, the other on the tonic A.
- Developments:
  - b252 – played in parallel 6ths (upper strings and woodwind)

- o b283 – used as a counterpoint to another theme in the violins
- o b315 – extended to 7 ½ bars
- o b322 – extended to 12 bars in diminished triads rising in parallel motion to a climax on G♭ b334
- 2nd phrase bb268-271: 2 × 2-bar question and answer phrases, mostly in semiquavers E major scales. One phrase ends on the dominant B, the other on the tonic E.
- Developments:
  - o b272 – repeated an octave higher, modified to sound like the dominant of A minor (i.e. C♮ instead of C#)
  - o b303 – repeated in B major (clarinet) and the dominant of A minor b311 (1st violin), alternating with the 1st (syncopated) phrase

Poco meno mosso bb346-377 – B♭ major, repeated 8-bar phrases in binary form (AABB), 32 bars in total.

- 1st phrase: angular opening bar followed by conjunct movement in the next
  - o Alternate tonic and dominant (B♭/F) first notes in each bar
  - o Decorated with appoggiaturas (b346^2 E♮ rising to F) and turns (b349^1)
  - o Dotted rhythms and staccato/legato markings give the same jaunty feel heard in the 2nd Dance (b96 onwards)
- 2nd phrase: more conjunct than the 1st phrase
  - o b363 – syncopated falling octave F's: ♪♩ ♪ becomes an important motif in the 5th Dance
  - o Switches between tonic minor (D♭'s bb362-365) and major (D♮'s bb366-369)
  - o Decorated with turns (b365) and grace notes (b369)

5th Dance bb421-450 – 2 contrasting *Allegro vivace* phrases:

- 1st phrase: 4-bar ostinato melody mostly in quavers, centred on A minor
  - o Quickly transposed to other tonal centres (E♭ b430 piccolo/oboe, D b433 viola, B b438 trumpets)
- 2nd phrase bb443-450: an exhilarating 8-bar melody in A minor, built from two 1-bar figures
  - o b443 – the syncopated falling octave motif heard in the *Poco meno mosso* (b363)
  - o b444 – mostly conjunct semiquaver runs
- Developments:
  - o b579 – syncopated octave D's are filled in with chromatic semiquavers
  - o b604 – syncopated octaves repeated 4 times by the whole orchestra in unison to end the piece

Tonality and Harmony	A variety of tonalities can be heard in this piece from several times and places:

Introduction

- b1 – opening melody is in **Dorian mode on A**
- b6 – 32nd note arpeggios outline the **Gypsy Dorian scale** on A with its distinctive raised 4th (ABCD#EF#G)
- b27 – in the key of A minor, with **19th-century Romantic** style chromatic chords and extensions:

Am   G$^{9(4\text{-}3 \text{ suspension})}$ F   E$^{7(4\text{-}3 \text{ suspension})}$ Dm^7 dim^{7th} Am^7/C   B$^{7(\flat5,9)}$

- bb37-40 – Impressionist style **chromatic non-functional** harmony:
  o | diminished 7th on A | C^7/ B♭ | dim 7th (A) | French augmented 6th (B♭DEG#) |

1st Dance

- Centred on E minor and moving to A minor, but the key is obscured by chromatic chords and the absence of conventional cadences, e.g. bb63-65: | Dm^7, G^7 | A^{sus4} | A major (**Tierce de Picardie**) |
- Extended chords, e.g. b66 dominant 9th on D, b68 G^{11} (no 3rd)
- Complete **circle of 5ths** in the bass underpinning the chromatic harmony, bb79-85
- b88-92 – **pedal point** on G with alternate concords and discords
- Perfect cadences are rare (bb81^2-82^1 V$^{7\flat,9}$-I in C major) and again avoided at the end of the section for continuity bb92-94:
  o | G | G/F | E♭ (which turns out to be V of A♭ minor)

2nd Dance

- **Functional harmony** confirming A♭ minor:
  o Dominant pedal bb93-99
  o bb100-102: | Augmented 6th (F♭)| Ic V^7 | I |

3rd Dance – D major

- **folk style drone** on D and A roots most of this section in D major
- mostly **diatonic** chords
- bb213-220 – sudden shift into E♭ major abruptly cancelled by functional harmony in D, with a circle of 5ths and V^7-I perfect cadence

4th Dance

- Begins on A minor, but the tonal centre shifts with increasing frequency as the section progresses, e.g. b268 E major, b276 D minor, b299 B, b307 E

	• Inner dominant pedal E bb236-247
	• Bare sounding harmony in **parallel 4ths and 5ths** bb299 and 307
	• Folk style drone bass on E and B bb264-275
	• 20th-century **quintal harmony** (chords built on 5ths instead of 3rds) bb258-262
	• bb322-334 – rising chromatic diminished triads over an F pedal; dominant preparation for B♭ major
	
	Poco meno mosso
	
	• B♭ major to start, confirmed by dominant inner pedal and ostinato tonic and dominant chords
	• bb362-369 – instead of following the harmony suggested by the B♭ major melody, Kodály reharmonises this in D♭ major before moving back towards the tonic. Again the expected perfect cadence bb368-369 is avoided with an interrupted cadence (F⁷- G♭⁷)
	• 20th-century style **atonal** link passage bb405-420 with a tritone ostinato bass (C and G♭)
	
	5th Dance
	
	• bb443-450 – repeated functional II-V-I progression in A minor, although the leading note G# is not present, giving a modal effect. However, the final two bars have a more tonal sounding Ic-V-I perfect cadence in A minor.
	• The II-V-I outline can also be heard in related keys, e.g. C major bb451-456, E minor bb459-464
	• bb502-505 – bare parallel 5ths
	• bb566-578 – Impressionistic chromatic non-functional harmony over a descending bass recalling the opening of the piece:
	  o b566 G#m/D#
	  o b569 E⁷/D
	  o b571 C#m
	  o b573 augmented 6th on C♮ (C♮EGA#)
	• bb604-607 – final syncopated octave E's and A's outline an emphatic final perfect cadence

Rhythm and Tempo	*Dances of Galanta* features a number of rhythm and tempo devices typically found in the verbunkos style and Hungarian/Gypsy dance music: • The tempo gradually speeds up over the course of the piece as a whole. Starting at *Lento* ♩ = 54, the tempo eventually reaches *Allegro vivace* ♩ = 152 at b421, and is even quicker from b579 • *Ritenuto* markings are used to emphasise expressive moments in the melody, e.g. on the quavers at b75 • *Stringendo* markings are used to create extra momentum and excitement, e.g. b326 • Sudden *animato* phrases interrupting the prevailing tempo, e.g. bb209 and 217

	• The dances are in either 2/4 or 4/4 time
	• Typical rhythms include:
	  o Double-dotted notes followed by 32nd note flourishes, e.g. bb1-4
	  o Lombardic or 'Scotch Snap' rhythms, e.g. the 3rd beats of bb50-52
	  o Syncopated figures followed by semiquaver runs, e.g. bb443-450
	  o March-like accompaniments with alternating on-beat bass notes and off-beat chords, e.g. 2nd Dance b93 onwards
	• Some 20th-century features are also present:
	  o Unusual time signatures, e.g. 1/4, b108
	  o Score is full of detailed markings for accents/staccato, e.g. 1st violin b443-450
	  o Impressionist style flexible tempi, pauses and 32nd note flourishes (Introduction bb1-49)

Texture	**Introduction**
	
	• bb1-18 – unaccompanied cello section solo, which then acts as a tonic pedal for the 32nd note flourishes in contrary motion (upper strings/flute). Rescored for solo horn b10, with cellos and piccolo joining in the answering flourishes.
	• bb37-43 – clarinet solo accompanied by rapid 32nd note arpeggios in contrary motion and multi-stopped pizzicato strings. Tutti climax at b43.
	• Clarinet cadenza bb45-49.
	
	1st Dance
	
	• Concerto style alternating solo and tutti sections:
	  o b50 – solo clarinet with homophonic strings and French horns
	  o b66 – tutti, with melody in flute, clarinet and upper strings plus sustained homophonic chords
	  o b74 – solo for clarinet, 1st violins and cellos with a lighter chordal accompaniment
	  o b82 – tutti, melody in lower strings and woodwind, with a slow march-like alternate bass/chords
	
	2nd Dance
	
	• b96 – solo flute with detached pizzicato string chords. Piccolo joins the flute melody and octave higher at b103
	• alternate tutti and solo sections
	• b129 – exotic rescoring of the melody on repeat:
	  o melody in parallel 4ths (flute/piccolo/2nd oboe)
	  o detached chords (pizzicato strings/muted trumpets)
	  o off-beat woodwind chords decorated with turns (1st oboe) and mordents (clarinets)
	• b151 – reprise of the 1st Dance now with melody played $f\!f$ across 3 octaves (upper strings/woodwind) with sustained chords (lower strings/woodwind/horns)

3rd Dance

- b197 – delicate high tessitura scoring:
  - o piccolo solo with clarinet countermelody
  - o *divisi* 1st violin harmonics, other strings play pizzicato
  - o glockenspiel and triangle outline the pulse and harmony
- bb205-216 – antiphony between woodwind and strings

4th Dance

- Syncopated 1st phrase in **parallel motion** in various intervals: octaves (b236 strings), 6ths (b252 1st and 2nd violins), 4ths (b299 trumpets/2nd violins)
- b258 – syncopated phrase heard in close **canon**; off-beat piccolo/clarinets lead, followed by on-beat horn 1 bar later
- folk-style drone **ostinato** accompaniments, e.g. lower strings bb248-282
- b283 – 2-part **counterpoint** between syncopated phrase (bassoon/viola/double bass) and a second theme (violins/cellos)
- b315 – both 1st and 2nd phrases from the 4th Dance heard together in counterpoint (woodwind semiquavers and strings/horns in close canon as before)

Poco meno mosso

- b346 – clarinet solo, with **detached ostinato chords**. Bass notes decorated with *glissandi* (bassoon/lower strings)
- b354 – theme rescored for bassoon/cello, with **arpeggios** added above the ostinato chords
- b370-385 – **imitation** of melody between upper strings and woodwind

5th Dance

- b421-442 – 4-bar ostinato melody played in **canon** between viola and 2nd violin, and then repeated in other entries as the texture builds. Accompanied by a **countermelody** b425 (flute/1st violin), sustained notes (horns/trumpets) and ostinato bass (timpani/lower strings)
- Frequent changes of texture to balance out the repetitive nature of the melodies:
  - o b443-450 – 1st violin melody doubled with fragments between the woodwind. Energetic semiquaver double-stopped string accompaniment.
  - o Folk-style 'oom-pah' bass/chord accompaniment (b451-466 lower strings/horns)
  - o bb467-470 – melody in bassoon and lower strings, with tutti off-beat chords
  - o bb471-474 – 2-part counterpoint between upper strings/woodwind, and trumpets/lower strings/woodwind

	• bb566-572 – 1st Dance theme passed between solo flute/oboe/ clarinet, with **pp** divisi tremolo 2nd violin/viola chords • bb602-607 – dramatic 2-bar silence followed by final heavily accented tutti octaves

Sample Questions

In Section A of the examination there will be one question on each of the two prescribed works. You must choose to answer **one** of these **two** questions (as well as a third 'musical links' question which will be discussed later). Here are four sample questions based on *Dances of Galánta* to use for practice. You may answer these in continuous prose or detailed bullet points and you should allow around 30 minutes under timed conditions to complete each question. Reference should be made to an unmarked copy of the score and remember to give precise locations for the musical features you discuss.

1. Béla Bartók once wrote, 'If I were to name the composer whose works are the most perfect embodiment of the Hungarian spirit, I would answer, Kodály.' Discuss this statement with clear reference to **at least three** passages in *Dances of Galánta*.
2. Discuss Kodály's use of melody and tonality in *Dances of Galánta*.
3. *Dances of Galánta* draws upon musical elements from both traditional Hungarian and Western cultures. Identify and explain **two (or more)** elements that have roots in traditional Hungarian music and **two (or more)** elements that originate from Western music.
4. Discuss Kodály's approach to rhythm and texture in *Dances of Galánta*. Refer in detail to specific passages of music.

LINKS BETWEEN THE PRESCRIBED
WORKS (HL ONLY)

Question 3 requires HL candidates to compare and contrast *Brandenburg Concerto No. 2* with *Dances of Galánta* with regard to one or two musical elements or concepts. This means you must write about similarities and differences in the use of, e.g. melody and rhythm between the prescribed works, taking care to ensure your points are relevant to the elements or concepts asked in the question. For example, in a question about Instrumentation, while it is true to state that both works contain keyboard instruments, this is not a significant musical link, but a comparative discussion of *how keyboard instruments are used in each work* is creditworthy in the IB examination.

The following table is a list of some of the musical links between *Brandenburg Concerto No. 2* and *Dances of Galánta*, along with the locations of possible examples. They are grouped together in musical elements with a brief outline of each link; you will of course need to add your own more detailed explanations – a useful revision task.

Comparative Links

Structure	Brandenburg Concerto No. 2	Dances of Galánta
Ritornello form, with shortened reprises of the main theme in different keys	1st movement, b1 (F major), b23 (C major), b56 (B♭ major)	1st Dance, b50 (E minor), b151 (A minor), b229 (Lydian Dominant scale on B♭
Complex structures using multiple forms	3rd movement: fugue b1, ritornello b47	b1 fantasia, b50 ritornello, b173 binary form, over-arching verbunkos form (slow bb1-235, fast bb236-607)

Themes/motifs used to unify the work as a whole	F-F-E motif, 2nd movt bb3³-4¹ violin heard earlier in 1st movt bb63⁴-64¹ flute	1st Dance used as a ritornello theme and reprised in the coda b567
Melody	**Brandenburg Concerto No. 2**	**Dances of Galánta**
Virtuoso solo parts	High tromba, 1st movt bb15-16	Clarinet cadenzas, bb44 and 573
Themes built from 2-bar phrases with repeats and variations	1st movt bb0⁴-8³, 2nd movt bb1³-3² and bb3³-5² (violin)	1st Dance bb50-65 (clarinet), 3rd Dance bb173-180 (oboe)
Decorated with ornaments and non-chord notes	2nd movt (violin): b3 trill and accented passing note (E), b4 suspension, b5 appoggiatura	Poco meno mosso: b349 turn (clarinet), b353 glissando (bassoon/cello), b369 grace notes (1st violin)
Longer notes in themes developed by filling them in with shorter notes	1st movt b86 violin: quavers of ritornello theme replaced with additional semiquavers	5th Dance (violins): syncopated motifs bb543 and 545 filled in with semiquavers in bb551 and 553
Diatonic melodies	1st movt ritornello theme bb0⁴-8³ F major	3rd Dance bb173-188 D major (oboe/flute)
Conjunct themes with a narrow range	3rd movt fugue subject bb1-6 tromba (1 octave)	2nd Dance bb96-108 flute (diminished 4th $G_\natural$ – $C_\flat$
Dissonant melodic intervals	2nd movt bb8³-9¹ flute (diminished 4th $G_\sharp$– C)	2nd Dance b111 1st violin (augmented 2nd $G_\natural$ – $F_\flat$
Harmony/ Tonality	**Brandenburg Concerto No. 2**	**Dances of Galánta**
Perfect cadences used to confirm keys	1st movt b8 (Ic-V-I in F major)	2nd Dance bb101-102 (Ic-V-I in $A_\flat$ minor)
Use of Interrupted cadences to avoid the finality of a perfect cadence and keep the music moving forwards	2nd movt bb62-63 (V-VI in D minor)	3rd Dance bb211-212 (V-VI in D major)

Extended chords	1st movt b51: Dominant minor 9th formed from D^7 chord and E♭'s in the melody (flute/oboe)	1st Dance bb66-69: dominant 9th on D, followed by G^{11} (no 3rd)
Complete circle of 5ths outlined in the bass	2nd movt bb49-56, starting and ending on A	1st Dance bb79-85, starting and ending on E♭
Chromatic harmony	1st movt bb107-112: sequence of dominant 7ths, diminished 7th on B (b112)	Introduction bb37-40: diminished and dominant 7ths, augmented 6th on B♭ (b40)
Tierce de Picardie	2nd movt b65 D minor key, ends with D major chord	2nd Dance b112 A♭ minor phrase ends with A♭ major chord
Tonic pedal to confirm the key	3rd movement bb136-139 (F)	3rd Dance bb173-209 (D)
Texture	***Brandenburg Concerto No. 2***	***Dances of Galánta***
Alternate solo/tutti passages	1st movt bb9-23	5th Dance bb506-518
Polyphonic textures	3rd movt bb 1–46 fugal opening	4th Dance bb303-321
Melody in bass parts	1st movt bb56-57 part of the ritornello theme (cello and violone)	Poco meno mosso bb354-361 (bassoon and cello)
Canonic imitation	1st movt bb87^4 cello and violone, followed by tromba 2 beats later	4th Dance bb276 upper strings and woodwind, followed by trumpets 2 bars later
Parallel motion used to develop melodies	1st movt b93^4 recorder and solo violin	2nd Dance bb123-133 woodwind instruments
Melody played in tutti octaves by whole orchestra	1st movt bb102^4-104 ritornello theme	Coda bb604-607 syncopated motif
Melody passed between solo instruments	1st movt bb9-22 1st concertino theme (violin, oboe, recorder, tromba)	Coda bb567-572 reprise of the 1st Dance (flute, oboe, clarinet)

Homophonic melody and chordal accompaniment	3rd movt bb135-139	1st Dance bb50-93
Rhythm	***Brandenburg Concerto No. 2***	***Dances of Galánta***
Syncopated ♪♩ ♪ motifs	3rd movt b10 tromba	5th Dance b443 1st violin
Phrases linked together by semiquaver runs	3rd movt bb15-21 tromba	5th Dance bb447-451 1st violin

Contrasting

Feature	***Brandenburg Concerto No. 2***	***Dances of Galánta***
Tempo markings	Movements have fixed tempo markings; 1st movt has no tempo indication	Greater variety of tempo markings and changes of tempo, e.g. bb 561–579 (stringendo, andante maestoso, allegro molto vivace, etc.)
Tonality	Major/minor keys, with modulations to closely related keys	Diverse range of tonalities and modulations to distant keys: b6 Gypsy Dorian mode, b50 E minor, b93 A♭ minor, b405-420 Atonality
Harmony	Mostly functional with some chromatic passages using dominant and diminished 7ths	More harmonic variety; b93 functional harmony, b37 non-functional harmony, b173 drone, bb66-69 extended D^9 and G^{11} chords

Sample Questions

In Section A of the examination there will be one compulsory question linking *Brandenburg Concerto No. 2* with *Dances of Galánta*. Here are three to use for practice. You may answer these in continuous prose or detailed bullet points and you should allow around 30 minutes to complete each question. Reference should be made to unmarked copies of both scores, and remember to give precise locations and explanations for the musical features you discuss.

1. Compare and contrast the use of harmony and tonality of each of the prescribed works, highlighting any significant musical links.
2. In what ways can both of the prescribed works be regarded as similar in their use of melody and melodic development?
3. Investigate significant musical links between the two prescribed works by comparing and contrasting their use of form and structure.

PRESCRIBED WORKS 2020–2021

RHAPSODY ON A THEME
OF PAGANINI (1934)
SERGEI RACHMANINOFF

Introduction

This Prescribed Work was composed by Sergei Rachmaninoff (1873–1943) at his villa in Switzerland during a rare break from his hectic performing schedule in the summer months of 1934.

The word 'Rhapsody' can be defined as an ecstatic expression of feeling, while the capricious nature of Paganini's original piece for solo violin could be described as mercurial and impulsive; these are all words which can be used to convey the character of this work, with its sudden and wide-ranging shifts of mood and displays of piano virtuosity which push the performer to the very edge of their technical abilities.

Rhapsody on a Theme of Paganini is a set of **variations**, a formal technique where musical material, often a melody, is repeated in a series of altered guises. These changes may involve melody, tempo, rhythm, harmony, texture, timbre, orchestration or any combination of these. One of the challenges posed by variation form to composers is managing the build-up of momentum and complexity while maintaining a sense of flow across the whole piece. Another question to consider is how far to depart from the original theme: staying too close risks too much repetition; stray too far and the listener will struggle to refer back to the original. Rachmaninoff's piece demonstrates how to control these factors successfully to create a masterpiece that has been a cornerstone of the repertoire since he gave the first performance with the Philadelphia Orchestra in Baltimore, USA, in 1934.

Instrumentation

The piece is scored for solo piano and the following Romantic period sized orchestra:

- Woodwind – 2 each of flute, oboe, clarinet, bassoon plus piccolo and cor anglais
- Brass – 4 French horns, 2 trumpets, 3 trombones and tuba
- Percussion – timpani, triangle, glockenspiel, snare drum, bass drum and cymbals
- Strings (1st/2nd violins, violas, cellos, double basses) and harp

Main Themes and Motifs

Rachmaninoff took his inspiration from two well-known themes: the primary theme comes from the *24th Caprice for solo violin* by the renowned virtuoso Niccolò Paganini; the melody itself proved an ideal basis for a composition and Rachmaninoff identified himself with Paganini's prodigious technical skill as a virtuoso solo musician.

- Simple AAB binary form with regular 4-bar phrasing and clear imperfect and perfect cadences in A minor. Rachmaninoff repeats the B section (AABB)
- A has a clear emphasis on the tonic and dominant of A minor; B features a descending sequence which uses a circle of 5ths to return to the tonic. When the melody is absent from a variation you will often still be able to hear these chord progressions
- Lively dotted rhythms and semiquaver flourishes

Rachmaninoff derives two motifs from Paganini's theme for development throughout the piece:

- A 5-note semiquaver figure bb1-2 which starts on the tonic A, leaps a third, then steps back to the tonic before leaping up a perfect 5th to the dominant E (ACBAE, motif *x*)

- Another motif with the same rhythm as *x* is the conjunct figure from bb9-10 which starts on the tonic and moves up to B flat before stepping down to F (AB♭AGF, motif *y*)

The secondary theme is taken from the first seven notes of the *Dies Irae*, a plain-chant melody from the Roman Catholic Requiem Mass. The ominous feelings of fate and dark shadows evoked by this melody fascinated Rachmaninoff and he used it in other compositions such as the *Isle of the Dead*. He felt it would make an effective contrast both musically and dramatically in connection with the Faustian legend that suggested Paganini traded his soul to the devil in exchange for his outstanding musical talents:

- Aeolian mode on A, also known as **natural minor** (G natural instead of G sharp)
- Narrow range of a perfect 4th, starts on mediant C before descending to the tonic A via an auxiliary note (B) and a double auxiliary note (B and G either side of the A's)

Together these themes provide not only the structure of the piece, but also its dramatic character.

Structure	The structure can be viewed on different levels. Not only as a single movement work lasting just over 20 minutes, but also as a set of 24 variations on Paganini's theme (numerically matching the 24th Caprice). Furthermore, the variations can be divided up into 3 sections broadly resembling the movements (fast/slow/fast) of a piano concerto: • Introduction up to Variation X • Variations XI to XVIII • Variations XIX to XXIV The following is an overview of the main characteristics and musical features of each variation. NB: instead of using the bar numbers for the piece as a whole, the bar numberings in this analysis are for each variation. **Introduction – 8 bars, A minor** • An arresting opening, with 4 × 2-bar sequential phrases, rising an octave each time • Orchestra play motif *x* harmonized with *f* detached chromatic chords, answered by the piano with strong accented tonic A's across 4 octaves • 2/4 time, Allegro Vivace • Final phrase is a sudden *p* perfect cadence leading straight into... **Variation I (Precedente) – 24 bars, A minor** • Unusually appears *before* the statement of the Paganini theme; this is because its skeletal outline flows into the theme and allows the music to build in complexity up to Variation V • Binary form AABB (4+4+8+8 bars) showing the simple underlying harmonic structure (tonic-dominant of A, descending sequence of B)

- Played by the orchestra alone in detached octave leaps, with the falling semiquavers from motif *x* for decoration on the repeat of B

Theme – 24 bars, A minor

- Played by violins with piano outlining harmonic skeleton heard previously
- More musical details can be found earlier on page 50

Variation II – 24 bars, A minor

- Rachmaninoff continues to keep the rate of change under control, e.g. same AABB phrase structure and light staccato scoring
- Theme in piano decorated first with grace notes; the repeat of B features rising and falling semiquaver arpeggios accompanied by falling chromatic triads in the upper strings

Variation III – 31 bars, A minor

- AABB phrase structure extended (6+6+9+10 bars)
- Only the chord pattern (tonic/dominant, descending sequence) is heard from the theme
- Motifs *x* and *y* are used in a busy, almost unbroken light semiquaver run shared between violins, flutes and later clarinets
- Piano has a contrasting legato part in quavers and crotchets with angular phrases in octaves

Variation IV – 40 bars, A minor

- Slightly faster tempo builds momentum
- Further phrase extensions (8+8+12+12)
- Based largely on motif *x*, which is explored through widening the original leap of a 5th sequentially (e.g. 1st 3 bars of piano RH: A-E, G#-E, F#-E)
- Motif *x* passed imitatively between piano and orchestra
- Original chord patterns can still be heard
- B section has a disjunct chromatic legato melody
- Imperfect cadence at the end segues neatly into…

Variation V – 36 bars, A minor

- Phrase structure is 4+4+14+14 bars
- Original chord patterns can still be heard, but more non-diatonic chords appear (e.g. b4 piano RH, F minor)
- Playful antiphonal interplay between short piano gestures featuring lower auxiliary notes and octave leaps, and accented syncopated detached orchestral chords
- Sudden dynamic changes (e.g. bb9-14, ***f*** and ***p***)

Variation VI – 54 bars, A minor

- Momentum of the dynamics and tempo built up in the preceding variations is interrupted for the first time
- Stop/start *poco rit./a tempo* markings
- Mostly *p* or *pp*
- New phrase structure: 7+7+16+12 bars, followed by a **coda** which recalls the opening A section of this variation
- A section harmony developed with piano playing rising 3rds outlining dominant E major while the orchestra pause on a *colla parte* instruction (b5 and 12)
- B section circle of 5ths decorated with chord extensions (e.g. bb15-19 A^7-D^9-G^{13}-C) and semiquaver chromatic part writing (e.g. b32 upper strings, b35 piano RH)
- Coda fades away with a rising tonic arpeggio in the piano, decorated with lower auxiliary notes

Variation VII – 42 bars, Aeolian on A

- A more ominous tone is created by the first piano statement of the *Dies Irae* theme in minim block chords
- Slower, moderate tempo
- Phrase structure is 8+8+10+16 bars
- bb1-16 are almost entirely in Aeolian mode but still centred on A
- Paganini theme is heard as a shadowy counterpoint in the orchestra
- Motif *x* used as a bass line (bassoon and pizzicato cello) in quavers, and imitative violin demisemiquavers (plus flute b41)
- Notice a fragmented statement of the B section in Violin I (bb27-36)

Variation VIII – 44 bars, A minor

- The impulsive energy of the Paganini theme returns at the original Allegro Vivace tempo
- More regular phrase structure: A 2×8 bars, B 2×14 bars, split into 8+6
- Paganini theme outlined in bold chordal octave staccato quavers rising up the keyboard (bb1-16)
- B section has a striking opening, with both hands playing chromatic chordal octaves split into staggered semiquavers (b17, repeated a tone lower b21)
- Antiphonal 1-bar exchanges between piano and orchestra at the end of the B sections are shortened to ½ bar, shortening the phrase to 6 bars (bb25-30 and 39–44)

Variation IX – 40 bars, A minor

- The momentum builds again as a **polyrhythm** is the main feature throughout

- Piano plays syncopated quavers against the quaver triplets of strings/woodwind/brass; both rhythms reinforced by percussion
- Phrase structure is 8+8+12+12 bars
- Texture and dynamics repeatedly build *p-f* with the phrasing before dropping back
- Piano textures alternate between octaves and large rising 8-part chords
- Paganini melody is largely absent, but its harmony can be traced (e.g. upper strings: tonic-dominant chords bb1-4, falling sequence of augmented triads b17 C#-F-A, then b21 B-E♭-G)

Variation X – 31 bars, A minor

- Marks the end of the first 'movement'
- Change of metre to 4/4; same tempo
- A section bb1-8: piano opens with *Dies Irae* in more forceful octaves, accompanied by the orchestra outlining tonic/dominant in a soft, detached march
- B section bb9-15: *ff* tutti climax with alternating jazzy syncopated 3/4 and 4/4 bars; *Dies Irae* heard in block chords as a descending sequence over a tonic pedal A
- B section b16-23: lighter scoring with *Dies Irae* in quaver triads split between piano LH/upper strings/glockenspiel, in counterpoint with motif *x* in constant semiquavers piano RH
- Coda b24: brass intone *Dies Irae* as piano/upper strings and woodwind cascade chromatically downwards in semiquavers over a tonic pedal in timpani and lower strings as the music fades to *pp*

Variation XI – 16 bars, towards D minor

- A transitional dream-like variation with a moderate tempo and softer dynamic
- Impressionist style with harmonic and instrumental colours:
- Non-functional extended chords (e.g. b3 C^6, b6 G^{13})
- 3/4 but no clear sense of metre
- Chromatic rising and falling piano cascades, like a written down improvisation
- Harp glissandi b15
- Only motifs from the Paganini theme remain (*x* in piano b3, 6 and 9; *y* in flute/cor anglais b10 and 12)
- Preparation for D minor can be seen in A dominant minor 9th chord over a D pedal (piano b14, harp b15, piano solo last 16 notes use *x* in rising sequence to outline this chord)

Variation XII – 32 bars, D minor (subdominant of A minor)

- A slow dignified but expressive 3/4 minuet
- AABB, 4 × 8 bar phrases
- Mostly diatonic harmony
- A section: simple rising legato melody outlining tonic and dominant passed between clarinets and horns; accompanied by piano counter-melody in dotted rhythms, pizzicato violins and harp chords
- B section: rising melody heard in descending sequence (note the expressive appoggiatura b20^1 cellos/horns). Repeat of B sees new melody in oboe using x on the upbeat b24^3 before horn takes over again on b28^3

Variation XIII – 24 bars, D minor

- Much louder, faster and forceful 3/4
- Paganini theme heard in string octaves with fewer changes and uses the 4+4+8+8 bar phrase structure heard in earlier variations
- Phrase endings feature striking syncopations, e.g. b4
- Piano accompanies the orchestra with powerful *ff* chords on the 2nd beat dropping to octave bass notes on the 3rd, most of which are D's giving a tonic pedal
- Surprise dominant chord substitutions, e.g. b4 expected A major chord is F# minor, and in b24^3 a C# minor chord (not C major) is used to jump into F major in the next variation

Variation XIV – 37 bars, F major (relative major of D minor)

- Loud and forceful again
- Paganini theme turned into a new fanfare-like melody with a falling triadic quaver triplet figure. Played by violins and upper woodwinds bb2^3-14, repeated by trumpets bb16^3-28
- The tonic-dominant (F/C bb2^3-6) and descending sequence (bb6^3-9) of the Paganini theme are still present
- Polyrhythm from Variation IX can be heard again, with the quaver triplets of the melody accompanied by straight quaver pairs
- **Hemiola** rhythms (e.g. bb24-27 2/4 metre across the 3/4 time signature)
- Piano silent until b14, then accompanies the melody with large block chords in both hands
- Chord substitutions continued from the previous variation (C#m-F instead of dominant C major, e.g. b3^3-4^1)

Variation XV – 57 bars, F major

- Technically demanding fast chromatic solo piano cadenza; orchestra joins in from b28
- A variation of the preceding variation! The triadic triplet figure becomes a 4-note semiquaver figure with an additional lower auxiliary note, and the hemiola rhythm can be seen with the slurs in bb10-11
- Triplet figure from Variation XIV is passed around the orchestra towards the end (b44³ oboe, later horn, clarinet and violas)
- Ends with a sudden soft piano F major chord, which is a dominant preparation for the next two variations

Variation XVI – 48 bars, B flat minor

- A little slower (Allegretto) and a return to 2/4 time, a graceful little dance with expressive melodies and light scoring
- Ternary form (ABA) with a 6-bar introduction:

Section A (bb7-22) with motif x in oboe
Section B (bb23-42), motif y in solo violin and clarinet
Short reprise of A (bb42-48)

- Chordal accompaniment in staccato quavers throughout along with shimmering demisemiquaver muted violins
- Section B has countermelodies (e.g. motif x in cor anglais b25, rising crotchet arpeggios in French horn b24, rising and falling piano figurations from b29)

Variation XVII – 25 bars, B flat minor

- A dark, brooding atmosphere
- Common time metre, but piano has 12/8 time throughout with a triplet feel
- Sliding chromatic movement in piano and tremolo strings
- Brass have long falling/rising gestures in octaves, joined later by woodwind
- In the last bar, Rachmaninoff transforms the mood with a harmonic shift onto an A♭ chord in readiness for the new key in the next variation

Variation XVIII – 42 bars, D flat major (relative major of B flat minor)

- The most famous passage of music in this work; an inspired, lush, romantic reworking of the Paganini theme
- Andante cantabile, 3/4 metre
- Entire Paganini theme is inverted, with motifs x and y on the upbeats often played *rubato*
- Played 3 times:
- bb1-13 piano solo, cadencing in the dominant **pp** building gradually to **f**

- bb13-24 orchestra accompanied by the piano, cadencing in the tonic with a *ff* climax
- bb24-42 counterpoint between piano and strings with a as the music calms down with a gradual *diminuendo* and falling chromatic harmony over a tonic pedal to a perfect cadence in D flat major

Link passage – 6 bars, moving back to A minor

- Returns to a vivace (lively) tempo
- Pizzicato strings, horns and bassoons announce the third 'movement' of the piece with a series of detached chords with sudden dynamic changes
- Widely spaced falling quaver triplet arpeggios in strings segue into the next variation
- The final 6 variations all showcase the virtuosity of the pianist, gradually building towards the climax at the end

Variation XIX – 20 bars, A minor

- A return to the mercurial mood from the beginning
- AABB phrase structure is 4+4+6+6 bars
- Common time, with a couple of 3/4 bars for rhythmic interest
- B section descending sequence still present bb9-11
- Piano takes up the widely spaced falling quaver triplet arpeggios heard in the link and plays them almost continuously through the variation in a pizzicato-like manner
- Accompanied by pizzicato string chords with *sf* accents, joined by clarinets and horn with crotchet triplets

Variation XX – 28 bars, A minor

- A little faster in tempo and rhythmic values (running semiquavers)
- Phrase structure is 5+5+9+9 bars; tonic/dominant A's and E's clearly present from the theme (piano bb2-3), as is the descending sequence (bb11-13 and 14-16)
- Piano has playful dotted rhythms throughout, mostly in octaves; orchestra have running semiquaver ostinato patterns (bb1-19 violins, then woodwind)
- Sudden dynamic contrasts *p* to *f*

Variation XXI – 20 bars, A minor

- A little faster again!
- Phrase structure is 4+4+6+6 bars; tonic/dominant A's and E's again present from the theme (piano bb1-3), as is motif *x* (viola bb1-3) and the circle of 5ths (cello bb9-12)
- Piano has quaver triplets in octaves throughout, but notes are sometimes grouped in chromatic pairs generating an exciting cross-rhythm, e.g. bb1-2:

- Lightly scored orchestral accompaniment with detached chords and occasional countermelodies (e.g. b15 flute and clarinet quavers, creating polyrhythm against piano triplets)
- Dramatic antiphonal chromatic chords in crotchet triplets between piano and orchestra (b4 and 8)

Variation XXII – 66 bars, A minor and E flat major

- The longest variation in the piece exploring motif x and the *Dies Irae*. Slightly faster once more, continuing to build momentum.
- AABB structure of the Paganini theme discarded in favour of an ABA[1] ternary form plus a piano cadenza:
  o Section A bb1-32: descending chromatic detached piano chords, each set starting progressively higher than the last. Accompanied by rhythmic and melodic fragments of motif x in strings and timpani. Sustained pedal A in double bass and bassoon. Notice from b23 the piano has the *Dies Irae* theme in a rising sequence of parallel diminished 7th chords
  o Section B bb33-45: pedal note changes to E♭; violins now take up the rising sequence, often using the auxiliary note figure from the first 3 notes of *Dies Irae* (e.g. bb35-37):

Piano has irregular rising and falling scales in octaves

  o Section A[1] bb46-65: as before but with piano arpeggios and an E♭ pedal
  o Piano cadenza b66: based on motif x, with rapid, powerful octave figurations

Variation XXIII – 53 bars, A flat minor and A minor

- 2/4 time, the AABB phrase structure returns after a 4-bar introduction which features a witty tonal conflict between A♭ minor in the piano, and home key of A minor in the orchestra as each forcefully tries to establish the key with $\boldsymbol{ff}$ octaves on the respective dominants
- Section A bb5-20: piano plays motif x $\boldsymbol{pp}$ in A♭ minor for 8 bars before being abruptly replaced by the orchestra playing it $\boldsymbol{ff}$ in the tonic A minor b12[2]
- Section B bb21-53: descending circle of 5ths from the theme is present (bb21-25 lower strings, first note of each bar is A-D-G-C-F), but disguised by falling chromatic chords, often syncopated
- Section B extends with more syncopated chords into another piano cadenza. Notice the inversions of motif x bb 41–42 upper strings and woodwind.

	Variation XXIV – 69 bars, A minor
	
	• Dominated by an extremely challenging piano part that even the composer struggled with!
	• bb1-2: piano RH has the tonic/dominant A's and E's in staccato triplet passages which leap up to 2 octaves, while the LH has widely spaced alternating bass notes and chords – all in a 6/4 polyrhythm against the 4/4 metre
	• b13: piano part changes to legato
	• Sparse orchestral accompaniment with fragments of motif *x*
	• Harmony is very chromatic throughout until b23 when A minor reasserts itself with V⁷-I perfect cadences (strings bb24⁴-25¹ and bb26⁴-27¹)
	• bb27-end can be thought of as a thrilling and spectacular coda which rounds off the piece with a climax:
	  o 2/4 time, even faster *Piu vivo* tempo
	  o tonic chord of A minor firmly established on every down beat of bb27-38, with a gradual crescendo
	  o b39 *Dies Irae* sounded in *ff* parallel motion block chords by strings and brass, in counterpoint with piano, woodwind and harp playing motif *x*
	  o b55 a switch to the tonic major as piano plays a cascade of semiquaver block chords split between the hands down the keyboard, accompanied by *ff* orchestral A major stabs which become syncopated
	• Final cadence has some playful unexpected twists:
	  o b63 tonic A pedal with rising chromatic triads up to a dissonant *sff* accented E♭ major chord
	  o Rachmaninoff dissipates all the energy with a cheeky *p* perfect cadence E⁷-A in open octaves using one last motif *x* (piano RH bb68-69)
	  o Notice the final A octaves suggest the final tonality is left unresolved – minor or major?

Melody	A wide variety of Variation techniques are on display across the whole piece for each of the main themes and motifs. Here are a few examples: **Paganini theme** • The whole melody is recognisably quoted in some variations: • Notes are removed to leave a simple harmonic outline in detached quavers (Variation I bb1-8 violins A's and E's) • Decorated with ornaments such as grace notes (Variation II piano bb1-16) and chromatic auxiliary notes (e.g. Variation II piano b1 A-G#-A, and b11 G-F#-G) • Change of time signature and rhythm (Variation XIII: 3/4, with the original dotted rhythms replaced by crotchets and quavers; also, the on-beat octave leaps of the theme are syncopated, e.g. bb4 and 8 strings and horns)

- Inversion, where in Variation **XVIII** the theme is turned upside down. In the comparison below notice how the melodic intervals and shapes of the variation move in the opposite direction to those of the original theme:

Variation XVIII

Theme

Motif *x* (ACBAE)

- When the whole theme is not used, this motif is present in almost all the variations as a way of unifying the whole piece by giving a link to the theme
- Introduction: the very first notes heard in upper strings and woodwind, repeated in rising octaves
- Variation III 1st and 2nd violins: bb1-4 *x* and its inversion (b1¹ CBAB) repeated in running semiquavers split between them; bb22 and 24 together in contrary motion
- Variation VII: used as a bass line to the *Dies Irae* theme (pizzicato cello, basses and bassoons); violins play soft, distant demisemiquaver reminders in counterpoint
- Variation X bb16-23 piano RH: *x* used to build a running chromatic semiquaver counterpoint to *Dies Irae*
- Variation XXII: the rhythm of *x* is used as a bass line in the timpani; *x* is also extended by adding the falling octave and the rising perfect 4th from the Paganini theme (ACBAEEA, bb4-5 violas) before being transposed and passed around the orchestra
- Variation XXIV: bb39-46 piano uses *x* in a sequence to outline the *Dies Irae* theme. Matching the Introduction, *x* is heard right at the very end of the piece (piano bb68-69)

Motif *y* (AB♭AGF)

- Not used as often as *x*
- Variation VIII bb31-33¹ piano RH: extra chromatic semitones are added between the main five notes to extend the motif
- Variation XI bb10-11 flute/cor anglais: a chromatic change which stays around G# and A instead of stepping down to F
- Variation XVI bb23-31 solo violin: an expressive chromatic variant centred around B flat minor

	Dies Irae (**CBCABGA**) • Variation X: bb1-8 (piano octaves) rhythmic diminution starting with all 7 notes of the theme in minims, then shortened to 3 in crotchets. Followed by syncopated quavers and crotchets across alternating 3/4 and 4/4 metres bb9-12 (piano, trumpets and trombones) • Variation XXII bb23-33 piano: rising sequence of parallel diminished 7th chords in 10 parts across both hands • Variation XXIV bb39-46: parallel block triads in strings and brass; arpeggiated quavers in woodwind, harp and glockenspiel; outlined in the piano using motif x in sequence
Tonality and Harmony	Although often hidden by some very chromatic harmony there is a clear tonal scheme running through the piece: • Introduction to Variation X – A minor • Variation XI – A minor moving to V of D minor (subdominant) • Variation XII and XIII – D minor • Variation XIV and XV – F major (relative major of D minor) • Variation XVI and XVII – B flat minor (subdominant of F major) • Variation XVIII – D flat major (relative major of B flat minor) • Variation XIX to XXIII – A minor • Variation XXIV – Rachmaninoff playfully leaves us guessing; A minor to start, but A major chords from b55, no 3rd in the final bar octave A's The tonal scheme is confirmed using some traditional harmonic devices: • Regular perfect cadences, e.g. Variation II b24 in A minor; Variation XII bb31-32 in D minor; Variation XVI bb40-41 in B flat minor; Variation XVIII bb23-24 in D flat major • Tonic pedal used to underpin chromatic harmony, e.g. Variation XXII bb1-32 A's in double bass, bassoon, tuba and timpani; Paganini theme original chord progression: • A section: Am | E | Am | E – simple alternation of tonic and dominant • B section: A | Dm | G | C | B^{dim} | Am | F^{#6} E | Am – circle of 5ths, followed by a diminished triad on B, an augmented 6th chord on F and a perfect cadence in the tonic Rachmaninoff's harmonic language in this piece is a mixture of different influences from different style periods: • Late Romantic extended chord progressions, e.g. Variation VI bb17-18: Am⁷ D⁹ | G¹³

	• Aeolian modal harmony on *Dies Irae* Variation VII bb9-15: Am | Em | Am | Dm | G | C | Am (reflects a 20th-century revival of ancient modes) • Baroque Neapolitan chord; Rachmaninoff often uses this as a substitute chord, e.g. in the key of A minor, a B flat major triad is used instead of the B^{dim} triad from the original, e.g. Variation II b21, Variation III b17, Variation IV b25, Variation V bb17 and 21 • Modern dissonant chromatic note clusters, e.g. Variation X piano bb24-25 • Impressionist non-functional extended chords create a dream-like effect, e.g. Variation XI piano: b3 C^6, b6 G^{13} (no 3rd), b9 A^7 plus a flattened 9th (B♭) and C naturals clashing with the C#'s • Neoclassical 'wrong note' harmony, e.g. Variation XIII b4 and 8: in D minor, the dominant A chords are replaced by F# minor • Rich Romantic chromatic chords approaching cadences, e.g. Variation XVIII piano bb23-24: in D flat major, F#m^{7b5} Ab^7 | D♭ • Impressionist style parallel chords, e.g. Variation XXII bb62-63: orchestra play repeated chromatic descending half diminished 7th chords on A#, A natural and G#

Rhythm and Tempo	*Rhapsody on a Theme of Paganini* features several rhythm and tempo devices which create both variety and momentum between the variations:
	
	• Allegro vivace (fast and lively) is the most common tempo in the piece, in keeping with the exuberant nature of the Paganini theme
	• *Piu vivo* (more lively) used to quicken the tempo into the next variation, e.g. III into IV, XIX-XX-XXI-XXII
	• A more moderate tempo is used to introduce the darker *Dies Irae* motif
	• Some variations feature one rhythmic device:
	  o Variation IX: a **polyrhythm** of syncopated piano straight quavers accompanied by quaver triplets in the orchestra
	  o Variation XX: piano plays dotted rhythms accompanied by running semiquaver ostinati in upper strings, later woodwind
	• Some variations are in a distinctive musical style:
	  o Variation XI: **Impressionist** style, with pauses breaking up the tempo, polyrhythms (piano b3, 6 and 9) elaborate piano arabesques in odd groupings (e.g. b10 has groupings of 8, 8 and 11 notes)
	  o Variation XII: a dignified **minuet** dance in 3/4
	  o Variation XIII: a 3/4 **waltz** with the piano emphasising the 2nd and 3rd beats
	  o Variation XIV: **hemiola** bb24-27, the 3/4 metre is disturbed by a 2/4 metre

	o Variation XXII: begins in a **march**-like 4/4 metre with a strict tempo, detached piano chords on each beat and motif *x* on the 4th beat of each bar (timpani and cellos)
Texture and Instrumentation	One of the outstanding features of these variations is the wide range of textures and timbres on display. There are too many to mention, but here are some variations which cover a range of examples: **Variation IV** • Close imitation of motif *x* – piano and cellos bb1-8, piano and flute bb13-16, piano and violins bb17-24 • bb9-16: piano RH melody is accompanied by wide LH arpeggios and detached chords in pizzicato strings • Counter-melody enters from b17 (cor anglais, 2nd violin) forming a polyphonic texture with the imitative motif *x* parts • b29 another melody is played by violins in legato octaves in a 2-part polyphony with the piano RH, lightly accompanied by pizzicato double basses • Contrary motion at the end (bb37-40) in piano and woodwinds **Variation X** • bb1-8: 2-part polyphony between the piano playing *Dies Irae* in *marcato* octaves and a march-like melody initially in the clarinet accompanied by detached chords. Gradual crescendo into… • b9: *ff* climax with a tutti chordal texture in parallel motion over a tonic pedal A in the bass instruments. Diminuendo into… • bb16-19: lighter *p* scoring featuring *Dies Irae* in chords split between on-beat upper strings and off-beat glockenspiel and piano LH in a high tessitura crossed above the RH, which plays motif *x* in running semiquavers. A further flute melody in long note values gives a total of 3-part polyphonic texture, accompanied again by a tonic pedal A in pizzicato double basses **Variation XVII** – a mysterious atmosphere is created with: • Low tessitura piano arpeggios mostly in parallel motion • Long legato calls from horns and trumpet in octaves (joined by woodwind b11) • Shadowy muted tremolo chromatic upper string chords in parallel motion at phrase ends, e.g. bb5, 9 and 22 **Role of the piano** Rachmaninoff was a world-renowned concert pianist, and although it is easy to view the *Rhapsody* as a vehicle for his own

considerable performing skills, the piano is used in the piece in a number of different ways:

- Rachmaninoff had an enormous hand span covering a 13th (an octave plus a 6th!), and there are passages where that was an advantage, e.g. Variation XXIV has frequent wide leaps which must be negotiated with speed and precision (b1-2 RH leaps increasing up to 2 octaves, also see b8 RH, b19-20 LH)
- The full range of the keyboard is used: Introduction b2 the lowest A is heard; Variation X b24 the descending chromatic arabesque starts on the highest A
- Virtuoso solo cadenzas, e.g. Variation XXII b66 based on motif *x*
- Accompanying the orchestra, e.g. Variation XVIII b133 melody in strings with piano block chords in triplets
- Variation XVII explores the darker timbres of the lower register before the tessitura gradually rises
- In Variation XXIII a dramatic and humorous argument with the orchestra takes place. Piano tries to establish A flat minor with dominant E♭ octaves b1, rebuked by the orchestra's E naturals b3 wanting to return to the tonic A minor. Although the piano plays the Paganini theme in A flat minor for a few bars, the orchestra again interrupts in A minor b12 and wins!

Sample Questions

In Section A of the examination there will be one question on each of the two prescribed works. You must choose to answer **one** of these **two** questions (as well as a third 'musical links' question which will be discussed later). Here are four sample questions based on *Rhapsody on a Theme of Paganini* to use for practice. You may answer these in continuous prose or detailed bullet points and you should allow around 30 minutes under timed conditions to complete each question. Reference should be made to an unmarked copy of the score and remember to give precise locations for the musical features you discuss.

1. The *Rhapsody on a Theme of Paganini* has been described as a cornerstone of the orchestral repertoire. Which aspects of the music make this piece so popular? Refer in detail to specific passages of music.
2. Analyse **three contrasting** passages of music to demonstrate Rachmaninoff's use of variation techniques.
3. Rachmaninoff was a great admirer of Paganini. What musical evidence is there in the *Rhapsody on a Theme of Paganini* to support this statement? Refer in detail to specific passages of music.
4. To what extent can the *Rhapsody on a Theme of Paganini* be regarded as a piano concerto? Make detailed reference to the score to illustrate your answer.

SYMPHONY NO. 94 IN G MAJOR
'SURPRISE' (1791)
JOSEPH HAYDN

Introduction

Joseph Haydn (1732–1809) was a celebrated Austrian composer of the Classical period. His innovations in the development of musical structure (especially Sonata Form), orchestral and chamber music led to him being called the 'Father of the Symphony' and 'Father of the String Quartet'.

Haydn spent much of his career as a court musician for the wealthy Esterházy family at their remote estate. In 1790 he became free to travel, and accepted a lucrative offer from Johann Peter Salomon, a German violinist and impresario, to stay in London to compose and conduct new symphonies (including this one) with a fine orchestra. This was a happy and productive time in Haydn's life and his music was popular in London before his arrival.

Haydn was known for his cheerful demeanour and sense of humour, and his love of practical jokes can be regularly heard in his music, especially this Symphony, which acquired its nickname from the sudden very loud chord in the 2nd movement intended to startle – and in some cases wake up – the audience! There are also a number of other musical jokes and surprises elsewhere in this piece.

Instrumentation

The symphony is scored for a typical late 18th-century Classical orchestra, which was much smaller than its modern counterpart:

- Woodwind – 2 each of flute, oboe, bassoon
- Brass – 2 French horns, 2 trumpets
- Percussion – 2 timpani (1 player)
- Strings (1st/2nd violins, violas, cellos, double basses)

The violins are given the lion's share of the melodic material, but Haydn also shares it around the woodwind, who by now were a well-established orchestral section. Brass and timpani were usually reserved for dramatically loud tutti passages and climaxes.

1st Movement: Adagio/Vivace Assai

Structure and Tonality	A lively, spirited Sonata Form movement in G major
	Slow Introduction bb1-17 (Adagio, 3/4 time)
	• In G major with some unexpected chromatic sequences before resolving onto a dominant pedal D
	Exposition bb18 (plus the preceding upbeat)-107 (Vivace assai, 6/8 time)
	• 1st subject bb18 (plus upbeat)-21^1 1st violin: opening G# in 2nd violin suggests Haydn is starting in the wrong key (A minor), but G major is quickly established
	• Transition bb21-79^1: already there is early development of the 1st subject (e.g. bb39-43 added countermelody, bb54-58 in D minor). Modulation to dominant D major b66
	• 2nd subject bb79^2-93 D major: 1st violin introduces the theme; b86 varied repeat with flute joining in
	• Codetta bb93-107^1: perfect cadence bb98-99 and tutti rising scale bb101-103 confirm D major, but instead of a clear final cadence, the music unexpectedly subsides into repeated 1st violin B's, which cleverly segue into both the Exposition repeat and the start of the Development
	Development bb107^2-154^1
	• Further exploration of motifs from the 1st subject
	• Passes through several keys: C major b107, F minor b115, D minor b125, B minor b141
	• Repeated 1st violin B's are again used to neatly segue into the Recapitulation
	Recapitulation bb154^2-257
	• 1st subject bb154^2-158^1 G major
	• Transition bb158-228^1: continued development of the 1st subject, mostly stays in G major
	• 2nd subject bb228^2-242 1st violin (plus oboe on varied repeat) in G major
	• Codetta bb242-257 modified this time to reach a final perfect cadence in the tonic G major

Melody	There are two main subjects/themes in this movement; both use crotchet and quaver rhythms in 6/8 and a typically Classical emphasis on the tonic and dominant notes of the scale.

1st subject bb18 (plus upbeat)-21[1] G major 1st violin:

- Starts on an upbeat with a rising perfect 4th B-E followed by falling conjunct movement to A; along with the G# harmony in 2nd violin implies wrong key of A minor
- Repeated in sequence a tone lower ending on G, establishing the tonic
- Rising in step via G# chromatic passing note up to C before falling in a diminished triad to cadence on the tonic
- Motifs: perfect 4th B-E; falling conjunct figure D-C-B-A; falling triad figure C-A-F#

Haydn explores the 1st subject and its motifs throughout this movement, not just in the Development section:

- Exposition: bb35-37 the falling conjunct figure now rises chromatically; bb39-43 falling conjunct figure added as a rising counter-melody (oboe)
- Development: bb107 in C major, perfect 4ths widened to 6ths; bb111-123 falling conjunct figure repeated through C major, F minor and D minor; falling triad figure used in B minor cadence b147 1st violins
- Recapitulation: bb195-198 falling conjunct figures (bassoons and lower strings) and falling triad figures (violins) combined in a descending sequence; bb206-209 violins have a rising figure built mainly from the perfect 4ths

2nd subject bb79[2]-93 D major 1st violin:

- Again starts with an upbeat; based strongly around the pitches of the tonic triad; starts on the dominant A, descends by step down to mediant F#; decorated with grace notes and trills
- Some wider falling minor 7th and octave leaps from high D b83-5, before cadencing on the lower D
- b86 varied repeat with flute joining in and a descending chromatic scale b88
- Motif: 3 repeated staccato quavers recur frequently in this melody; used as the link between Exposition repeats and start of both the Development and the Recapitulation (bb105-107 and 152–154 1st violins)

Harmony	As with all the movements in this Symphony, many of the typical Classical harmonic features can be heard here: • Mostly diatonic with occasional chromatic chords • Predominance of chords I and V, e.g. bb21-29 in G major; bb66-73 alternating I and V^{7}b chords in D major • Regular cadences to confirm keys, e.g. Ic-V^7-I D major bb85-86 and 92-93 • Pedal points in the bass: bb21-29 tonic pedal in G major; bb107-118 dominant pedals in C major followed by F minor • Dominant chords usually extended with a 7th (b30^2 V^7 in D major, b50-53 V^{7}b in A major), and sometimes a striking flattened 9th (b115 V^{b9} in F minor CEGB♭D♭) • Occasional chromatic chords: diminished 7th heard in a rising sequence bb10-12; augmented 6th b119 D♭FA♭B♮
Rhythm and Tempo	• Slow *Adagio* tempo in 3/4 b1, changing to a fast *Vivace assai* ('very lively') 6/8 metre • Repeated quaver pulses and semiquaver runs frequently drive the music along, e.g. bb21-34 • Dance-like accompaniment with accented *fz* syncopation bb66-73 lower strings
Texture	• Melody-dominated homophony is the main texture in tutti passages, another important feature of the Classical style, e.g. bb21-34 There are also frequent changes of texture for variety and interest: • The 1st subject is usually presented with a light 2- or 3-part polyphonic texture, e.g. bb18-20, 39–42 • Tutti orchestra in octaves, e.g. bb101-105 • Close rhythmic imitation bb195-198 between bassoon/lower strings and violins

2nd Movement: Andante

Structure and Tonality	Theme and Variations in subdominant key of C major (Andante, 2/4) **Theme** bb1-32 • Binary form AA^{1}BB^1, regular 8-bar phrases • C major apart from brief modulations to dominant G major in the A sections (bb8 and 16) • The section repeats are slightly different: A^1 has the famous surprise *ff* G major chord b16; B^1 has flute and oboe joining in with the melody • Ends on a perfect cadence in the tonic

Variation I bb33-48

- Binary AABB with exact repeats, C major
- The surprise chord is now at the start of A
- Added counter-melody in 1st violins (plus flute at the end of A)
- Ends on a perfect cadence in the tonic

Variation II bb49-74

- Louder, stormier variation in C minor (apart from a brief modulation to its relative E flat major b56)
- B section is replaced by a passage where A is developed (notice the quaver triad motif in lower strings and bassoons bb57-60)
- Different ending: imperfect cadence in C minor bb68-69, 1st violins then have a link passage based around the dominant G chord which segues straight into...

Variation III bb75-106

- Returns to C major
- Oboe solo b75 doubles the theme's quaver note pairs to 4 semiquavers
- Lighter scoring, especially b83 onwards with only violins playing the theme against a flute/oboe 2-part counter-melody often in 3rds and 6ths
- Ends on a perfect cadence in the tonic

Variation IV bb107-142

- C major, a type of **double variation**, where each A and B section are treated differently:
  o A b107 – a f tutti with theme in brass and upper woodwind, violin semiquaver triplets and off-beat chords
  o A^1 b115 – p strings and bassoon with theme in dotted rhythms; off-beat chords continue
  o B b123 – p, similar to A^1
  o B^1 b131 – f, similar to A, with additional fanfare-like rhythms, e.g. b132
- Ends on a perfect cadence in the tonic, but extends straight into a 4-bar bridge which pauses dramatically on a diminished 7th chord on F#

Coda bb143-156

- A quiet ending, based on A but reharmonised with diminished 7th chords over a C tonic pedal

Melody	The main theme for the following variations is a simple violin melody which allows room for development as the movement progresses:
	• C major, AA¹BB¹ phrase structure, 4 × 8 bars
	A section

	• Main motif is the repeated staccato quaver pairs moving in arpeggios which mostly outline the tonic and dominant of C major
	• Classical style regular **question and answer phrasing**, e.g. bb1-2 rising tonic arpeggio; bb3-4 same rhythm, but falling dominant arpeggio
	• Brief modulations to G major b8 with falling octave, and b16 with a rising octave
	B section
	• More disjunct bb17 and 19, centred on dominant G
	• Quaver arpeggios return b21
	• Cadence decorated with a **turn** figure around B b23
	• Repeated with flute and oboe joining in
	Variation I
	• Theme unchanged (2nd violins), but a counter-melody added in the 1st violins; features falling semiquaver pairs which form suspensions (4-3 b35¹) and appoggiaturas (b36); B section counter-melody has chromatic lower auxiliary notes, e.g. b44 F# and D#
	Variation II
	• Section A heard in C minor string/woodwind octaves, modulating to E♭ major
	• B section replaced by development of main quaver pair motif from A:
	o Sequential imitation between lower strings and bassoon bb57-60
	o Extra notes added to the quaver pairs bb61-62 violins
	o Quicker dotted rhythms bb66 and 68 strings
	o Used as a link into next variation bb73-74
	Variation III
	• Quaver pair motif doubles into semiquaver fours bb75-82 oboe
	• Repeat of A treated differently; violins play theme against a 2-part flute/oboe counter-melody

	• B melody is modified to act as a harmony to the continuing flute/oboe counter-melody (e.g. bb95-98 violins) **Variation IV** – double variation: • Section A melody in *ff* trumpet/horn along with upper woodwind; repeat is shared between violin dotted rhythms (bb115-116) and lower strings/bassoon quaver pairs (bb117-118) • Section B violins decorate the melody with dotted rhythms and semiquaver appoggiaturas; repeat melody grandly returns to trumpets/horns with some fanfare rhythms (e.g. b132) • Bridge to the Coda based on quaver pairs, but now in threes **Coda** • Based on Section A melody but reharmonised with diminished 7th chords
Harmony	• Almost entirely diatonic with occasional chromatic chords • Predominance of chords I and V, e.g. bb1-32 in C major (G major bb7-8 and 15–16) • Regular cadences to confirm keys, e.g. V^7-I G major bb7-8 and 15-16; V-I C major bb23-24 and 31-32 • Pedal points in the bass: bb145-156 tonic pedal in C major • Occasional chromatic chords: diminished 7th on F# heard on the tutti pause b142^2
Rhythm and Tempo	• Andante tempo and 2/4 metre throughout • Regular *tenuto* markings (emphasise note by holding for its full length) on crotchets at phrase ends • Variation II: exciting demisemiquaver scales and energetic dotted rhythms • Variation IV: rhythmic layers create textural interest quaver pairs, semiquaver triplets and syncopated chords bb107-114; tutti fanfare rhythms bb132 and 134
Texture and Scoring	This movement has some interesting changes of texture and instrumentation in each variation: **Theme** • Simple 2-part melody and bass line bb1-8 • Melody and detached chords bb9-16 including the famous *ff* chord with triple-stopped violin chords adding to the effect • More legato flute/oboe parts double the melody along with a sustained horn dominant inner pedal – a contrast to the more staccato strings **Variation I** • 2-part polyphony (2nd violin theme and 1st violin/flute counter-melody) with light chordal accompaniment

Variation II

- A section: melody in string/woodwind octaves, alternating with melody and broken chords bb49-56
- b57 has a more layered texture with quaver motif imitated in lower strings/bassoon, sustained chords in flute/oboe and rapid violin scales passed between 1st and 2nd violins

Variation III

- Melody and staccato broken chords bb75-82
- Light scoring with melody in unison violins and a 2-part counter-melody in flute/oboe b83; joined by sustained horns b99

Variation IV

- Rhythmic layers create textural interest b107: quaver pairs in brass woodwind and timpani, 1st violin semiquaver triplets, and syncopated multi-stopped string chords

Coda

- Oboe/bassoon melody with sustained chords in strings and horns

3rd Movement: Menuetto/Trio Allegro molto

Structure and Tonality	A 3/4 dance-like movement in G major with thematic links between the Minuet and Trio. The structure can be discussed on two different levels:
	<ul><li>Overall a ternary form (ABA = Minuet-Trio-Minuet); the reprise of the Minuet is usually performed without repeats</li><li>The dances themselves both have 2 repeated sections which suggest an AB binary form, but given the B sections contain a modified reprise of the A sections, it is best to regard these as being in **rounded binary form** | A | BA^1 | (each half repeated)</li></ul>**Minuet** bb0^3-62^2<ul><li>A bb0^3-18^2 – tutti featuring a melody with mostly crotchets; modulates to dominant D major; repeated</li><li>B/A^1 bb18^3-62^2 – B starts with imitative quaver scales before passing through several keys (G minor, E flat major, C minor) via a harmonic sequence before settling on the dominant D major in preparation for the reprise of A^1 b40^3 in G major and modified to stay in the tonic</li></ul>**Trio** bb62^3-89^2<ul><li>Lighter scoring of ***p*** strings and bassoon</li><li>C bb62^3-70^2 – opens with an inverted version of the quaver scales from the Minuet Section B; modulates to D major; repeated</li></ul>

	• D/C¹ bb70³-89² – opens with the same melody as C; like the Minuet passes sequentially through keys (C major, D major, E minor) before settling on the dominant D major in preparation for the reprise of C¹ b80³ in G major and modified to stay in the tonic **Minuet *da capo*** • *da capo* b89 means go back to play the Minuet again, thus ending the whole movement at b62²
Melody	All the themes start with an upbeat, and consist mostly of crotchet and quaver patterns. This movement is a good example of Haydn's skill in motivic development: **Minuet** • bb0³-8 1st violin and flute: Classical style 2 × 4-bar question and answer phrases, outlining tonic and dominant 7th arpeggios of G major, mostly in crotchets • Motif: the opening 3-note scale G-A-B is used at the start of all the other themes in this movement • bb8³-18: explores an auxiliary note figure decorated with a grace note (b9); repeated as a sequence • Motifs: the 6-note scale b16 and the arpeggio figure b17 are used in the other themes in this movement:  • bb18³-40 violins: built almost entirely from the 3 motifs mentioned above; all 3 are heard in succession at the start of this section; arpeggio figure is used in a modulating sequence bb28-34; 3-note scales are playfully imitated in rising and falling solos bb38³-40 **Trio** • bb62³: opens with an inverted version of the quaver scale motifs from the Minuet Section B; the C# is an appoggiatura • Motif: the disjunct F#-D-F# crotchet figure b64 is developed as a rising sequence bb72-76
Harmony	• Almost entirely diatonic with occasional chromatic chords • Predominance of chords I and V, e.g. bb0³-8 and 35-62 in G major • Regular cadences to confirm keys, e.g. V⁷-I D major bb17-18; V-I in G major bb53-54 • Notice the V chord has no 3rd in b53 – D⁵ with no F#, a folk music influence • Pedal points in the bass: bb54-62 tonic pedal in G major • Dominant chords usually extended with a 7th (b4 V⁷ in G major, b9 V⁷ of C major)

	• Modulating sequence bb28-35: series of V^7-I progressions in G minor, E♭ major, C minor and the dominant D major; the melody also adds a 9th to the dominant chords, e.g. b28^2 violin E♭ adds a flattened 9th to the D^7 chord
Rhythm and Tempo	• Strict tempo and 3/4 metre throughout • Tutti pause b48 • All the phrases are anacrusic (begin with an upbeat)
Texture	• Mostly melody-dominated homophony with contrasting textures and scoring in new sections • Tutti melody and chords bb0^3-18^2 • Imitation of auxiliary note figure bb13-15 between higher and lower instruments • 2-part imitation between upper strings and lower strings/bassoon bb18^3-24 • Contrasting chordal textures bb28-34: sustained woodwind against detached multi-stopped strings • Parallel 3rds bb48^3-52 violins, oboes and bassoons • Lighter scoring in the Trio: bb62^3-70 1st violin and bassoon melody in octaves with detached string chords; bb70^3-75 2-part violin polyphony over a simple lower string bass line

4th Movement: Finale Allegro di molto

Structure and Tonality	This fast, capricious Finale (2/4, G major) to this symphony is in **Sonata-Rondo** (ABACABA) form; popular in the Classical period, this is a hybrid structure with features from both Sonata Form (Exposition, Development, Recapitulation) and Rondo Form (recurring main theme with episodes between).

A	B	A	C	A	B	A
Exposition			**Development**	**Recapitulation**		
1st subject I	2nd subject V	1st subject I	Various keys	1st subject I	2nd subject I	1st subject I

Haydn, like many composers, does not stick to this 'textbook' table, and typically weaves in a few musical 'jokes' along the way.

Exposition bb0-153 – 2 subjects: 1st in G major, also the main Rondo theme; 2nd in the dominant key D major

• 1st subject bb0-37 G major
• Episode bb38-74 G major modulating to D major, develops motifs from the 1st subject

- 2nd subject bb75-87 D major
- Episode bb87-103 D major back to G major; note the false ending at b99!
- 1st subject bb103-111: a short reprise in G major, interrupted by another...
- Episode bb111-145: further development of 1st subject motifs, G major, arriving at B minor (but never confirmed by a cadence!); segues into...
- 1st subject bb145-153, yet another short reprise in G major but leading straight into...

Development bb153-181

- Effectively another episode; continues to explore 1st subject motifs passing through G minor, B flat major, settling on to a dominant pedal D in preparation for the...

Recapitulation bb181-268

- 1st subject bb181-209 G major
- 2nd subject bb210-225 also now in G major
- 1st subject bb225-268: a short *p* reprise, but interrupted by a *f* timpani roll which heralds the final drive towards the thrilling climax of both the movement and the Symphony as a whole

| **Melody** | Again, all the themes start with an upbeat, and here consist mostly of quaver and semiquaver patterns. This movement is another good example of Haydn's skill in motivic development: |

1st subject/Rondo theme:

- Entirely diatonic in G major
- 2×4-bar question and answer phrases: bb0^2-4 centred around the notes of the tonic triad; bb4^2-8 same rhythm but centred more on the dominant before falling in a scale to the tonic
- Motifs (in brackets): the opening 3-note semiquaver rising arpeggio upbeat; the 3 repeated quaver G's b2; the syncopated falling quaver pairs over the barline of bb2-3

The theme and its motifs are developed throughout the movement. Here are a few examples:

- b31: upbeat omitted but used 2 bars in a row bb34-35; modified ending bb36-38 with original scale replaced by a falling minor 7th down to leading note F#, resolving to the tonic G
- b58-63: first 2 bars of theme quoted as a sequence in D major
- bb75-85 2nd violin: semiquaver arpeggio figure accompanies the 2nd subject

	• bb120-145 all 3 motifs are used in this Episode:
	  o syncopated quaver pairs bb120-129 woodwind and lower strings
	  o semiquaver arpeggio now a 3-note falling scale bb129-131 woodwind and lower strings
	  o the 3 repeated quavers used in the cellos and basses (bb131-135), and by 1st violin with an additional wide leap (bb132-135)
	  o semiquaver arpeggio now chained together in rising 1st violin phrase (bb138-139)
	• bb155-159 strings: repeated and syncopated quaver motifs combined in a rising sequence
	• bb173-174 1st violin: syncopated quaver pairs now repeated in disjunct falling leaps

Harmony	• Mostly diatonic with occasional chromatic chords • Predominance of chords I and V, e.g. bb0-16 in G major; bb43-52 in D major • Regular cadences to confirm keys, e.g. V^7-I G major bb4 and 7-8 • Repeated tutti V-I cadences to emphasise ends of sections, e.g. bb94-99 in D major; bb259-268 in G major to end the Symphony • Unresolved Ic chord in B minor bb138-142 eventually segues into reprise of the main theme abruptly back in G major. Another of Haydn's musical jokes • Pedal points in the bass: bb75-83 the 2nd subject is underpinned by a tonic pedal in D major • Chromatic chord progression bb65-66: Key D major: | G#^{dim}/B Gm/B♭ | D/A F/A | • Chromatic augmented 6th chords: b135 GBDE# resolving to Ic of B minor (F#BD); b171 E♭GB♭C# resolving to V of G minor (DF#A) • Near the end the tonality threatens to move away from the tonic on a surprise E♭ 1st inversion chord b234
Rhythm and Tempo	• Strict very fast tempo and 2/4 metre throughout • Tutti pauses are marked by silent bars to maintain the pulse, e.g. bb74 and 209 • All the main themes are anacrusic (begin with an upbeat) • Repeated quaver pulses and semiquaver runs frequently drive the music along, e.g. bb64-71 and 242-261 • Repeated syncopated passages with *fz* accents, e.g. bb163-172, more frequent from b173-174 with diminution

Texture	• Melody-dominated homophony is the main texture in this movement, another important feature of the Classical style, e.g. bb0-37
	• The 2nd subject is softly scored with the melody in the 1st violins doubled by oboe and flute and a light chordal accompaniment with pizzicato cellos and basses
	• Reprises of the 1st subject are often approached with a monophonic 1st violin line, e.g. bb143-145 using the semiquaver arpeggio motif; bb179-181 semiquavers running straight into the main melody
	• Timpani roll starting ***p*** b226 suddenly becomes ***f*** b233 as the tonality threatens to move away from the tonic on an E♭ chord – another Haydn surprise!

Sample Questions

In Section A of the examination there will be one question on each of the two prescribed works. You must choose to answer **one** of these **two** questions (as well as a third 'musical links' question which will be discussed later). Here are four sample questions based on '*Surprise*' Symphony to use for practice. You may answer these in continuous prose or detailed bullet points and you should allow around 30 minutes under timed conditions to complete each question. Reference should be made to an unmarked copy of the score and remember to give precise locations for the musical features you discuss.

1. Discuss Haydn's use of form and tonality in the **1st movement** of the '*Surprise*' Symphony.
2. Haydn was known for his love of musical jokes and surprises. What musical evidence is there in the '*Surprise*' Symphony to support this statement?
3. Discuss Haydn's approach to melody in the '*Surprise*' Symphony. Refer in detail to specific passages of music.
4. Explain how Haydn's '*Surprise*' Symphony is typical of a work from the Classical period, illustrating your arguments with precisely located examples.

LINKS BETWEEN THE PRESCRIBED WORKS (HL ONLY)

Question 3 requires HL candidates to compare and contrast *Rhapsody on a Theme of Paganini* with *Symphony No. 94 'Surprise'* with regard to one or two musical elements or concepts. This means you must write about similarities and differences in the use of, e.g. melody and rhythm between the prescribed works, taking care to ensure your points are relevant to the elements or concepts asked in the question. For example, in a question about Instrumentation, while it is true to state that both works contain brass instruments, this is not a significant musical link, but a comparative discussion of *how brass instruments are used in each work* is creditworthy in the IB examination.

The following table is a list of some of the musical links between *Rhapsody on a Theme of Paganini* and *Symphony No. 94 'Surprise'*, along with the locations of possible examples. They are grouped together in musical elements or concepts with a brief outline of each link; you will of course need to add your own more detailed explanations – a useful revision task.

Comparative Links

Structure	*Rhapsody on a Theme of Paganini*	*Symphony No. 94 'Surprise'*
Theme and Variation form, with main theme musically altered in each variation	The entire piece, 24 variations	2nd movement, 4 variations
Complex structures using multiple forms	24 variations can be grouped together to form 3 'movements' of a piano concerto (I-X fast, XI-XVIII slow, XIX-XXIV fast)	3rd movement ternary form overall (Minuet-Trio-Minuet), but separately the Minuet and Trio are both in rounded binary form

Unifying themes and motifs heard at the start and used throughout	Paganini theme, and motif *x* (ACBAE)	4th movement 1st subject or rondo theme, and the rising semiquaver arpeggio motif (DGB)
Melody	***Rhapsody on a Theme of Paganini***	***Symphony No. 94 'Surprise'***
Diatonic themes, outlining tonic and dominant triads	Theme bb1-8 violin (I and V of A melodic minor)	3rd movement bb1-8 violin (I and V of G major)
Regular phrasing in binary form	Theme bb1-24 AABB, 4+4+8+8 bars	2nd movement bb1-32 AA^{1}BB^1, 8 bars each with varied repeats
Themes built from motifs with repeats and variations	Theme derived from dotted rhythm and motif *x* (ACBAE) bb1-2	2nd movement theme derived from quaver pairs moving in arpeggios bb1-2
Decorated with ornaments	Variation II grace notes (bb1-16 piano)	3rd movement grace notes (bb9-15 violins); 1st movement trills (2nd subject bb80 and 82 violins)
Variation techniques	***Rhapsody on a Theme of Paganini***	***Symphony No. 94 'Surprise'***
Change of rhythm	Variation XIII: 3/4 crotchets and quavers, syncopation at phrase ends	2nd movement Variation II dotted rhythm b68; Variation III oboe semiquavers bb75-82
Change of major/minor mode	Variation XVIII in D♭ major	2nd movement Variation II in C minor
Counter-melodies added	Variation VII: *Dies Irae* (piano) in counterpoint with motif *x* (bassoon)	2nd movement Variation I: 1st violin/flute melody in counterpoint with theme (2nd violin)
Double variations	Variation II: grace notes bb1-16; theme split between flute and clarinet bb17-24	2nd movement Variation III: oboe semiquavers bb75-82; flute/oboe counter-melody bb83-106

Harmony/Tonality	Rhapsody on a Theme of Paganini	Symphony No. 94 'Surprise'
Perfect cadences used to confirm keys	Theme bb23²-24, and Variation II b24 (both V⁷-I in A minor)	3rd movement bb17-18 (V⁷-I in D major), bb88³-89 (V-I in G major)
Use of Imperfect cadence to avoid the finality of a perfect cadence and keep the music moving forwards	Variation IV bb40 (chromatic progression ends on V of A minor, segue into Variation V)	2nd movement bb68-69 (Ic-V in C minor, followed by a link passage into C major)
Extended chords	Variation XVIII b23³ V¹³ in D♭ major	1st movement bb115 V♭⁹ in F minor CEGB♭,D♭
Modulating sequences	Theme bb17-20 passes through D minor and C major	3rd movement bb28-35 passes through G minor, E♭ major, C minor and D major
Augmented 6th chord	Theme bb15¹ and 23¹ implied by outline F-D# leap	4th movement b171 E♭,GB♭,C# resolving to V of G minor
Tonic pedal to confirm the key	Variation X bb24-31 (A minor)	3rd movement bb54-62 (G major)
Texture	Rhapsody on a Theme of Paganini	Symphony No. 94 'Surprise'
Antiphony	Variation VIII bb25-30 piano and orchestra	1st movement bb1-9 woodwind/horns and strings
Melody-dominated homophony	Variation XVIII b13³ onwards	1st movement bb21-34
Polyphonic textures	Variation XVI bb33-42 solo clarinet theme plus 2 counter-melodies in piano RH, harp and cello	1st movement bb39-42 3-part polyphony between 1st/2nd violins and oboe
Imitation	Variation IV bb1-8 piano, with violas 1 beat later	2nd movement bb57-60 cellos/basses, with violas and bassoons 1 bar later
Parallel motion used to develop themes	Variation VIII bb1-15 piano both hands in 3rds and/or 6ths	2nd Movement bb107-114 brass and woodwind instruments in 3rds and 6ths

Melody played in tutti octaves	Variation I	1st movement bb101-106; 2nd movement bb49-52
Humour/Jokes	***Rhapsody on a Theme of Paganini***	***Symphony No. 94 'Surprise'***
Use of dynamics	Variation XXIV ends cheekily on a **p** V⁷-I cadence after a huge **ff** tutti *crescendo*	2nd movement b16 the famous sudden **ff** chord after a **pp** phrase
Tonality	Variation XXIII bb1-12 piano (A♭ minor) and orchestra (A minor) 'argue' over which key the music should be in	1st movement upbeat to b18 1st subject starts in the wrong key (A minor) before resolving to tonic G major b20

Contrasting

Feature	***Rhapsody on a Theme of Paganini***	***Symphony No. 94 'Surprise'***
Tempo markings	Greater variety of tempo markings and changes of tempo, e.g. Introduction Allegro vivace, Var. VII Meno mosso, Var. XV Piu vivo etc.	Movements have fixed tempo markings; occasional pauses, e.g. 2nd movement b142
Tonality	Wider range of tonalities and modulations away from A minor to distant keys: Var. VII bb1-16 Aeolian mode, Var. XVI B♭ minor, Var. XXIII A♭ minor	Major keys, with modulations to closely related keys, e.g. dominant
Harmony	More harmonic variety; Theme functional, Var. VII modal, Var. XI non-functional harmony, Var. XXIV chromatic	Mostly diatonic and functional with a few chromatic chords (augmented 6th and diminished 7th) and passages (2nd movt bb145-153)

Sample Questions

In Section A of the examination there will be one compulsory question linking *Rhapsody on a Theme of Paganini* with *Symphony No. 94 'Surprise'*. Here are three to use for practice. You may answer these in continuous prose or detailed bullet points and you should allow around 30 minutes to complete each question. Reference should be made to unmarked copies of both scores, and remember to give precise locations and explanations for the musical features you discuss.

1. Compare and contrast the use of harmony and tonality of each of the prescribed works, highlighting any significant musical links.
2. In what **musical** ways do the prescribed works both exhibit a lively character and sense of humour?
3. Investigate significant musical links between the two prescribed works by comparing and contrasting their use of Theme and Variation form.

Section B

PERCEPTION AND ANALYSIS OF MUSICAL STYLES

This chapter will give all musical features of each style that is often featured in this part of the examination. It is not possible to cover every eventuality here – there has been a vast amount of music created across world history – but it is possible to learn and revise the most important styles and the terminology associated with them. The IBO breaks these styles down into three main areas: Western Classical Music, Jazz and Pop, and World Music. Remember that for this examination, Western Classical Music spans a period running from 1550 up to the present day – not just the style that emerged in Vienna at the end of the 18th century. The dates that are used for the different periods of Classical Music are not absolute; the Baroque period did not start the day after the Renaissance period ended! It is best to think of musical styles and periods overlapping, constantly evolving and developing over time, with the dates given to indicate when certain methods and approaches to creating music were in vogue.

WESTERN CLASSICAL MUSIC

Renaissance Period (1550–1600)

Key features

- Most Renaissance music was written for voices, either for church services and ceremonies (sacred) or for secular (i.e. non-church) purposes such as private entertainment or dancing.
- Melodies are based on **modes**, but composers gradually added more accidentals. This is the start of the evolution towards major and minor keys established in the Baroque period. Most melodic movement is **conjunct** (step-wise); where there is a leap, it is almost always followed by a step back in the opposite direction.
- Textures tend to be **polyphonic**, with melodic lines **imitating** and weaving around each other. However, you will also hear some **homo-phonic** phrases. Composers also liked to have passages where one group sang or played, followed by an answering phrase from another group. This is called **antiphony** and should not be confused with 'call and response', a term used to describe similar passages in African drumming or Blues.
- Harmony consists mainly of **root-position** and **first-inversion** chords, and composers also used **cadences** to round off sections or end pieces. As well as **perfect** (V–I) cadences, expect to hear **plagal** (IV–I, or 'Amen') and **imperfect** cadences, which always end on chord V. Sometimes a piece in a minor mode will end on a major chord – this is known as a **Tierce de Picardie**.
- Other popular harmonic devices were the result of melodic lines interacting with each other. The most common example of this is the **suspension**, but another very distinctive effect was the **false relation**.
- Many Renaissance works are through-composed. This means they are based on a succession of ideas (points) which in sacred music were often discussed polyphonically – hence the term 'counter-point'. Other important structures were Variations in keyboard works, binary forms in dances and strophic form in lute songs.

Genres, contexts and composers

Church music to begin with was sung in Latin and intended to be sung *a cappella* (unaccompanied), and consisted mainly of **masses** and **motets**. The mass was a setting of parts of the rite of Holy Communion to music, and motets were based upon a few verses from the Bible and sung during the service or on special days in the Church year. But the Reformation, in the dual form of the Church of England and the Catholic Council of Trent, had an influence on music for worship in two significant ways. Firstly it was decreed that the words should be more easily heard, which meant an increase in the use of homophonic textures and solo voices at the expense of polyphony. This was a musical trend that continued into the early Baroque period. Secondly the Elizabethan regime demanded new sacred music to be written in English, so that everyone could understand the words. This gave rise to new genres such as the **anthem**, like a motet but sung in English and sometimes accompanied by organ. In the examination you may be able to tell which language is being sung, and the mass movements all begin with the same key words (Kyrie, Gloria, Credo, Sanctus, Benedictus and Agnus) so it is worth remembering them as they will enable you to identify the genre accurately. Possible composers include Palestrina (Italy), Byrd and Tallis (both England).

In Venice, the sacred music performed at St. Mark's Cathedral made great use of its architecture. There were two choir galleries each with an organ built high into the opposing walls of the church. Giovanni Gabrieli was probably the finest composer of **polychoral** music, and often wrote for three or more groups using combinations of voices and ceremonial instruments such as trombones and cornetts (a wooden trumpet with a brass mouthpiece).

The most important secular vocal genres were the **madrigal** and the **lute song (ayre)**. Madrigals originated in Italy and were written for a varied number of voice parts, usually one with one singer on each part. They were mostly unaccompanied and the texts were poems about love or satire, and were a popular form of self-entertainment in royal and aristocratic circles. Madrigals became a genre where composers such as Monteverdi and Gesualdo felt they could freely experiment with new rhythm, melody and especially harmony, in their efforts to fully express the meaning of the text. Some of their music was controversial because of the strong dissonances they used, something which led Monteverdi to suggest there should be two separate ways of writing music: one for the church (*prima prattica*) and another for secular society (*seconda prattica*). Their popularity spread to Elizabethan England where Byrd, Weelkes and Morley also used vivid word-painting to illustrate their poems. Ayres were often strophic in form and were usually performed by a solo voice with the lute accompanying; the most famous Renaissance musician across the courts of Europe in this genre was the English lutenist and composer John Dowland.

In the Renaissance, instruments were secondary to voices, and they were mainly used for ceremony, dances and accompanying vocal music. Many instrumental pieces were simply transcribed from vocal pieces, but some original works were created. Variations were composed for a harpsichord-like instrument called the virginal, and dances were written for consorts (groups) of viols (a family of bowed string instruments) or crumhorns (double-reeded woodwinds like an oboe). A popular pair of dances was the **pavane and galliard**; the pavane was a stately dance in 2, while its partner was a livelier dance in 3. Like most dance music they had repeated sections, a constant tempo and periodic phrasing.

Baroque (1600–1750)

Key features

- To begin with, textures were thinner and more homophonic (melody and chords). This was known as **monody**. However, polyphonic textures came back as the period went on.
- The **continuo** was the foundation for most genres of Baroque music; this consisted of a bass part (mostly cello but sometimes bassoon) and a keyboard part (harpsichord or organ) improvised chords from figures written below the bass part – hence the term **figured bass**. This is probably the most recognisable feature of Baroque music.
- Above the continuo parts, melodies were often written in long, winding phrases decorated with **ornaments** such as trills, mordents and turns.
- Baroque pieces often only have one **affection** (mood) running from beginning to end. Contrast in the music was achieved by pitting a few instruments against many, or by alternating loud and soft sections (**'terraced dynamics'**) – note that *crescendo* and *diminuendo* were rarely used.
- Viols were gradually replaced by the violin family. This was the era of the great violin makers of Italy, such as Stradivarius. The violin, viola, cello and double bass formed the first complete section of the orchestra as we know it today. Woodwind (flute, oboe and bassoon), trumpets and timpani (kettle drums) were sometimes added to the strings and continuo.
- By around 1700 the Greek modes used in the Renaissance were reduced from seven down to just two – Ionian and Aeolian, or major and minor. The French composer Rameau produced the first book about harmony and tonality, and J. S. Bach wrote his '48' Preludes and Fugues, two of each in every possible major and minor key.

- Several new structures evolved alongside **binary** (AB) form: **ternary** (ABA, especially in *da capo* aria), **rondo** (ABACA), **ritornello** (used frequently by Vivaldi in his concertos) and **fugue**, a type of piece using polyphonic texture.

Genres, contexts and composers

The Baroque period in music took its name from the ornate style of architecture that was in fashion. It was a time of experimentation and many new musical genres were developed. It is customary to divide the 150-year period into three blocks of fifty:

1600–1650	Early Baroque (Monteverdi, Schutz)
1650–1700	Mid-Baroque (Corelli, A. Scarlatti, Lully, Purcell)
1700–1750	Late (or High) Baroque (Bach, Handel, Vivaldi)

You should try to familiarise yourself with the sound of each sub-period, as this will help you to date the music you hear more precisely.

The late Renaissance concept of seconda prattica, where the words were more important than the music, gave rise to monody, a solo voice with simple continuo accompaniment. The rhythms were composed to match as closely as possible the natural accents of speech and melodies were designed to emphasize the meaning of the words (or 'word painting') with dramatic leaps and chromatic dissonances. This style of singing was called **recitative**, which became the most important way of conveying dialogue and storytelling in **opera**. The first operas in the early 1600s were based on ancient Greek stories and tragedies and consisted of little else but recitatives, but Monteverdi soon realised the genre needed more variety and added short choruses and instrumental pieces. Towards the end of the 17th century composers coupled their recitatives with **arias**, a more poetic, song-like piece where the character could reflect or expand upon their situation as suggested by the preceding recitative.

Opera spread as a popular theatrical entertainment from Italy to France and England. Lully's operas for the court of King Louis XIV at Versailles featured dances and what became known as the French Overture, an orchestral introduction to the opera with a slow section full of dotted rhythms followed by a fast section often with a fugal opening with the parts entering at different points with the same (or modified) theme. Henry Purcell's *Dido and Aeneas* featured French and Italian influences, as well as some distinctively English features such as the use of Ground Bass in some arias. At the end of the 17th century Alessandro Scarlatti was developing the *da capo* aria and the Italian Overture. The *da capo* aria was cast in ternary form but written in binary (AB) with an instruction to repeat the first section, and the Italian Overture had three sections (fast–slow–fast) and would later go on to form the basis of the Classical Symphony. At the end of the Baroque period Handel was the best known opera composer and many of his works were premiered in London.

The church still had a significant influence on society at this time, to the extent that opera was not permitted in theatres during holy seasons such as Lent. Instead they put on **oratorios**, which re-told Bible stories without staging or costume, but in musical terms they are difficult to distinguish from opera – both contain overtures, recitative and aria, and choruses. The greatest oratorios of the Baroque period were composed by Bach and Handel, thus it is most likely that you will hear the words being sung in German or English. Bach was also well known for his **cantatas** (a form of miniature oratorio), which he wrote for the services at his churches in Leipzig, Germany.

During the Baroque period instrumental music gained more importance. A popular new genre was the **trio sonata**; 'trio' was a reference to the number of parts in the score, two melody lines and a figured bass part. But remember that continuo involves two players, a bass and a keyboard instrument, which actually makes a total of four players. There were two different types of trio sonata: **sonata da camera** (to be played in a room at home) and **sonata da chiesa** (for use in church), but they are both essentially **suites** of dances. These dance movements were almost always in the same key, cast in a Binary form which depended on the same tonal structure, with the A section moving from tonic to dominant, and the B section wending its way back to the tonic via a series of related keys. The best known composers of trio sonatas were Corelli, Couperin, Bach and Handel. Although the number of movements could vary, there were four dances that were usually present in trio sonatas:

- Allemande – a German dance in 4/4 time and a moderate tempo.
- Courante (running) – a French dance in 3/2 or 6/4 and a fairly fast tempo.
- Sarabande – a slow stately dance from Spain in 3/4, with an accent on the second beat.
- Gigue (Jig) – a fast French/English dance in a compound time such as 6/8.

Another important new genre was the **concerto**, either in the form of a **concerto grosso** (for a group of soloists, orchestra and continuo) or a solo concerto. The idea of contrasting groups in Baroque orchestral music can be traced back to the antiphonal pieces of Giovanni Gabrieli at St Mark's, Venice. Corelli, Bach and Handel are again notable composers in this genre, but the most important composer here is Vivaldi, with his distinctive driving rhythms and flowing melodic lines. Vivaldi taught violin at an orphanage for girls in Venice and most of his concertos were written for recitals by the orchestra he formed there. In a concerto grosso the solo group – typically two violins and a cello – was called the **concertino**, and the main body of strings and continuo (around twenty in number) was known as the **ripieno**. Many concertos had three movements (fast–slow–fast), and a popular structure for the fast movements was the **ritornello**, literally meaning 'return', because the main **tutti** (played by all) theme would re-appear at regular intervals in related keys. In between these *ritornellos* there would be contrasting solo sections for the concertino or single soloist, accompanied by the continuo.

Fugue can be regarded both as a genre and a texture. It is a polyphonic piece based on one main theme (called the **subject**) which is then imitated between the different parts (voices). At the start of a fugue the voices enter one by one using the subject. When all have entered, the opening section (**exposition**) has concluded. What follows is a series of episodes (freer material sometimes derived from the subject) and **middle entries** of the subject in related keys. The fugue ends with the final entries in the tonic key. Fugues can be vocal or instrumental and can appear in all of the other genres mentioned previously, either as a self-contained movement or as part of a larger movement, in which case it is known as a **fugato**. All the mid- and late Baroque composers wrote fugues, but the outstanding composer here is J. S. Bach, who wrote many for harpsichord and organ in particular, and he would often pair them with a prelude (literally an introductory piece) or a toccata (a piece featuring rapid and skilful finger work). **Tip:** when you hear a fugue, try to listen out for the order in which the voices or parts enter.

Classical (1750–1810)

Not to be confused with 'Classical' in the record shop sense, where it is used to refer to music across all the style periods discussed here. This period features the music of Haydn, Mozart and the early works of Beethoven.

Key features

- A far greater use of **homophonic textures** than the Baroque. **Melody and chords** is very common, and pieces were lighter and clearer than the weightier polyphonic sound of the Late Baroque. However, polyphonic textures do still exist in this period, so do not assume too much!
- Classical music sounds **elegant, polished** and **well balanced** in both its phrasing and structure. As in all music there is expression and emotion, but here it is always kept in check by its structure.

- Within the bounds of the structure, Classical pieces had a **wider range of contrast and variety**. Composers would write different sections of their music in different moods by contrasting the keys, themes, rhythms and dynamics.
- Melodies are usually **shorter** than their spun-out Baroque counterparts, centred around the tonic and dominant triads and have clear **question and answer phrases** marked by **cadences**.
- Harmonies are still **diatonic**, but some chromatic chords are creeping in, such as **diminished 7ths** and **augmented 6ths**. Devices such as **pedal points** become more common.
- Dynamics had now developed into a more dramatic set of instructions, such as **crescendo/diminuendo** and **sforzando**.
- The harpsichord continuo filling in the chords for the Baroque orchestra was made obsolete by the development of the Classical orchestra's **wood-wind section** (2 each of flutes, oboes, clarinets and bassoons).
- The harpsichord was also no match for the **piano**, with its ability to play at different dynamics. A very typical piano texture to listen out for was **Alberti Bass**, a type of broken chord accompaniment.
- New forms of instrumental music evolved, many with a sonata-like multi-movement format, e.g. **symphony**, **string quartet**, **sonata**, **concerto**.
- **Sonata Form** is the most significant new structure. Not the form of a *whole* sonata but a *single movement within* that sonata! Remember – **exposition** (themes presented in contrasting keys)**, development** (themes developed/explored/combined in several keys)**, recapitulation** (all themes restated in home/tonic key only).

Genres, contexts and composers

Some significant changes were afoot during the Classical period. For the first time, all the significant composers were based in one part of Europe, namely Austria and Germany. For a time these composers were all based in the city of Vienna and this marks the start of what can be seen as a domination of Western music by this region. Instrumental music was for the first time more important than music for voices. Although the **piano** became fashionable in the second half of the 18th century, it had been invented at the end of the 17th century. Unlike the harpsichord's keys which were plucked, the piano's keys were struck by hammers, and the amount of force and touch used on each key could be varied to create dynamic contrasts, smooth **legato** or detached **staccato** styles of playing. Many piano sonatas were written by Haydn, Mozart and Beethoven, mostly for entertaining small audiences in aristocratic households, but other purposes gradually evolved; some were written for playing for pleasure at home, while some of Beethoven's later works are on a grand scale more appropriate to the concert hall as the pianos became bigger and more powerful in design. Indeed, it was not only the aristocracy who would listen to live music – the emerging **middle class** had disposable income which they could spend on attending concerts, opera and even their own instruments. This in turn changed the very nature of the composer's employment; Haydn was one of the last composers to hold a court position, and Beethoven was the first truly freelance composer writing music commissioned by a variety of patrons. Many of Beethoven's symphonies and concertos were premiered at subscription concerts. Furthermore, with more people owning and playing instruments, a new market arose for music that was playable in the home: music for piano, voice and small chamber ensembles.

The **symphony** can be thought of as a 'sonata for orchestra' and they grew out of the Baroque Italian overture because they were usually in three sections (*fast–slow–fast*) which became separate movements. Haydn is usually credited with adding a Minuet and Trio after the slow movement to complete the familiar four-movement format we know today:

1st movement – Allegro (fast) in tempo, sometimes preceded by a slow Introduction – usually in Sonata Form.

2nd movement – Adagio (slow), often more lyrical – structure can be ABA (Ternary), Theme and Variations, or Sonata Form.

3rd movement – Minuet and Trio (fairly fast, 3/4 time) – a dance movement which Beethoven later changed to the faster Scherzo.

4th movement – Allegro, usually light and joyful in mood – structure can be a Rondo (ABACA), Sonata Form again, or a hybrid Sonata-Rondo (ABA–C–ABA – the two ABA's are equivalent to the Exposition/Recapitulation and the C is the 'Development' section).

It is worth learning these designs as it will enable you to discuss the wider structure and context of the fairly short CD extract you may be given. Other genres such as Trios and String Quartets also had four movements in this layout. Sonatas and Concertos often only had three of these movements, with the Minuet omitted.

The Classical **Concerto** is a continuation of the Baroque solo concerto with two new features, the double exposition and the cadenza. The **double exposition** is a modification made to the first movement's sonata form structure; the orchestra and soloist each have their own exposition – the orchestra play first, followed by the soloist accompanied by the orchestra. After this the development and recapitulation follow as usual, but near the end of the recapitulation, the orchestra pauses on a Ic (tonic 2nd inversion) chord. The soloist plays the **cadenza**, a virtuoso passage based on the main themes where s/he can display their technical brilliance. The pre-arranged signal for the end of the cadenza is a trill, at which the orchestra come in again to round off the movement with a coda. Cadenzas are often improvised but some composers preferred to write their own.

A large amount of chamber music was written mainly for home entertainment, and it is worth noting a couple of points here. Firstly, whereas the Baroque trio sonata actually required four players, from the Classical period onwards the ensemble name equals the numbers of players. By the end of the period Beethoven had composed a Septet (seven players), and the early Romantic composer Schubert an Octet (eight); both sound like small-scale orchestral works, but are still capable of an intimate sound. The **string quartet** came to be regarded as the perfect chamber music combination (2 violins, a viola and a cello), and Haydn was credited with creating the musical template followed by later composers. A feature of quartets to watch out for is the *frequent changes in texture* as a means of maintaining musical interest.

Classical works also started to become known by their 'nicknames', usually describing something heard in the piece. Haydn's symphony No. 94 was called 'The Surprise' because of the sudden fortissimo chords in the quiet second movement, and Mozart's string quartet K.465 was known as 'Dissonance' because of the remarkably chromatic introduction to the first movement.

Opera in the late Baroque period had reached a point where the singers held too much creative control; music was written for them to show off their vocal skills at the expense of the action and the storytelling. In the 1760s Gluck composed operas that redressed this imbalance with music that fitted and reflected the action, and more continuity from recitative to aria, often merging the two. The finest operas written in this period are all by Mozart (*The Marriage of Figaro, Don Giovanni, The Magic Flute*). Mozart's operas took the genre to a new level, with music written to match every subtle change in the drama or the characters, not just for the singers but for the orchestra as well.

Beethoven (1770–1827)

You will notice from Beethoven's dates that they fall across both the Classical and Romantic periods – and this is also true of his music. As mentioned earlier he was the first freelance composer and inspired the Romantic composers after him. It is usual to divide up his music into three periods:

First period – similar in style to Haydn and Mozart (Beethoven had some lessons with Haydn in Vienna). Symphonies 1 and 2, String quartets 1–6, Piano sonatas 1–12 (there are 32 in all).

Second period – Classical forms modified and expanded. Music is on a much grander scale and has more impact, drama and conflict. Orchestra became larger and included piccolo, double bassoon and trombones. Symphonies 3–8, 'Razumovsky' quartets, the 'Moonlight' sonata comes from this period. His deafness was on the increase.

Third period – these works were composed entirely in his aural imagination; he was by now totally deaf. The 9th Symphony (the first ever to feature voices and bass drum, cymbals and triangle), the late quartets and piano sonatas.

Romantic (1810–1900)

Although all composers look to express themselves through their music, the Classical style balanced this out with the importance attached to structure and form. In the 19th century however, this balance was clearly shifted towards expressiveness.

Key features

- **Lyrical melodies**, often using more chromaticism. Key changes became more distant from the Tonic; earlier periods modulated to the dominant and relative minor, but mediant, or third-related key changes (e.g. from B major to G major) were popular in the Romantic period.
- Harmony also became more **chromatic**, with **extended chords** (9ths, 11ths and even 13ths) and strong **dissonances**, all of which started to undermine the tonal system established in Baroque times.
- Following Beethoven's lead, the Romantic orchestra is much larger than before. A fully fledged **brass section** became possible with the introduction of **valves**. More strings and woodwind were often needed to match the power of the brass.
- Huge diversity in the range of different genres; from short 2-minute songs and piano miniatures up to 4-hour operas.
- Closer links to art and literature led to the development of **programme music** inspired by fantastic and imaginative stories, poems and paintings. Classical forms were modified and altered to fit with the programme, and **recurring themes** were used to hold the large-scale pieces together.
- Great increase in technical skills and **virtuosity**, particularly in piano and violin. Some Romantic pieces were considered unplayable when they were first published!

Genres, contexts and composers

The German **Lied** was a song written for solo voice and piano – not just an accompaniment here, but an equal partnership, often cleverly creating the mood and drama of the poem with its own preludes, interludes and postludes. Most Lieder were either strophic (same music for each verse) or through-composed (different music for each verse). The best known composer here is Schubert; he wrote over 600 Lieder, including 9 in one day. They range from the dramatic chase of *Erlkonig* (The Erlking) to the lost love of *Ihr Bild* (Her Portrait). Sometimes songs were grouped together in 'song-cycles' with a theme or story behind them. Schumann and Brahms were also notable Lieder composers.

Piano music evolved rapidly during the 19th century thanks to advances in its design and the abilities of the players. An iron frame was introduced, allowing greater tension on the wires, giving a wider dynamic and tonal range, further enhanced by the soft pedal. Chopin and Liszt exploited these advances to the full, writing preludes, stirring waltzes and serene nocturnes (literally 'night music'). Chopin was known for the influences of his native Poland (e.g. mazurkas) and his melodic **arabesques**, Liszt for his astounding virtuosity (e.g. *Grand Galop Chromatique*) but also moments of reflective beauty. Again Schumann and Brahms are counted among the greatest of the Romantic pianists. Many middle-class households owned a piano and a wide variety of music that could be played for personal pleasure was published.

Programme music (i.e. music that tells a story or paints a picture) was a very important feature of Romantic orchestral music written for the concert hall, and composers made full use of the new forces at their disposal. Many one-movement works called either concert overtures or tone poems were created. Mendelssohn's *Fingal's Cave* is an overture which evokes the wild coasts of Scotland, while Richard Strauss' *Till Eulenspiegel* tells through music the medieval tale of a practical joker and trickster who is eventually hanged for his crimes. On an even bigger scale the 5-movement *Symphonie Fantastique* by Berlioz takes the listener through several different dreams the protagonist had had about his beloved; a waltz at a ball, and the March to the Scaffold where he is beheaded for a crime of passion, to name but two. In the examination you will only be played a short extract from these large-scale pieces, but there are good marks for structure and context to be scored if you can display some wider knowledge beyond what you can hear. For example, most programme music relies upon a recurring, or motto-theme, to inform the listener of what is happening. This theme is then transformed and developed as the piece progresses in ways that accurately fit the drama or imagery with, for example, new rhythms or ornamentation.

The rapid rise in the technical virtuosity of solo performers led to an increase in the difficulty composers put into their concertos. Some of these were initially regarded as being impossible to play (e.g. Tchaikovsky's *Violin Concerto*). Many composers also regained creative control of the cadenza by writing their own instead of leaving it up to the soloist. As with other orchestral genres, there were experiments with the structure of movements, perhaps linking them together, or merging the movements into one continuous piece.

The two main countries for Romantic opera were Italy and Germany. Once again there was a trend away from separate numbers towards a more continuous music, integrating recitative and aria, sometimes lasting across a whole Act. Giuseppe Verdi is considered one of the greatest opera composers; his characterisations were subtle and expressive and the drama he created through his music was both direct and intense. Among the most popular of his operas is *Aida*, set in Ancient Egypt. Richard Wagner took the idea of integration to an extreme with his '**music-dramas**'. He preferred this name to 'opera' as he aimed to produce music for the stage which involved all of the Arts. A very large orchestra played a significant role in Wagner's music-dramas, but its size and power posed a major problem for the singers. To enable them to be heard more clearly Wagner had a theatre specially built at Bayreuth, Germany, with the orchestra housed in a large pit below stage level. Among his finest achievements was the *Ring Cycle*, a series of four operas based on the legends of the Norse Gods. Each of these operas were 3–4 hours long, and in order to keep the audience informed of the action Wagner devised a system of **Leitmotifs**, giving each character, object or place its own unique themes. These melodies were woven into the music to show when, for example, a character was on stage or being referred to, and were modified to reflect their situation or mood.

During the 19th century, a group of composers sought to break away from the dominant German musical influences of the period by using the folk melodies and dance rhythms from their own countries in their compositions. This movement became known as **Nationalism**. The first nationalist composers came from Russia and were known as the 'Mighty Handful' after their powerful orchestral works. Of these the best known are Mussorgsky (*Pictures at an Exhibition*) and Rimsky-Korsakov (*Scheherazade*). In Bohemia (present-day Slovakia and the Czech Republic) Dvorak's *Slavonic Dances* used the local dances such as the polka and furiant, while Smetana's *Vltava* is a tone poem that traces the course of the River Vltava all the way to Prague. Other countries with nationalist composers were Norway (Grieg), Finland (Sibelius) and England (Vaughan Williams). Sibelius and Vaughan Williams, along with the Russian Shostakovich and the Hungarian Bartok ensured the nationalist movement continued well into the 20th century.

Modern (1900–Present)

Up until 1900 the periods of music history could be regarded as having one style which was largely common to all of its composers. But the Modern period has seen an ever-increasing and exciting diversity of different styles, influences and experiments. There are some common musical trends which will be mentioned first, but thereafter it is easier to treat 20th-century music one style at a time.

Key features

- The dominance of major–minor tonality was broken by **atonality**, a new system which treated all the notes of the chromatic scale as equals, with no sense of tonic and dominant. Other tonal systems evolved, such as the **whole tone scale**, and older systems such as modes were revived.
- Melodies were more likely to be disjunct rather than conjunct, sometimes with extremely dissonant wide leaps.
- Harmonies were no longer subject to tonal relationships, so they became more dissonant and were also used purely for their effect.
- There was a more vibrant and energetic use of rhythm, with cross rhythms, polyrhythms, odd time signatures, sudden changes of metre and accent.
- The changes of approach to rhythm were coupled with both the expansion of the percussion section in the orchestra and an increasing use of ethnic percussion instruments.
- There was a never-ending search for new timbres. Composers looked to use traditional instruments and voices in new and unusual ways, or use newly invented instruments; and with the advent of sound recording and synthesis, it became possible to shape and create sound like never before.

Impressionism

A style with links to the visual art of painters such as Monet, musical impressionism was first created by the French composer **Claude Debussy**. Like many forward-thinking composers, he was looking for a new direction away from the excesses of late Romanticism. In the same way that Monet blurred the outlines of his pictures, Debussy blurred the outlines of his music by avoiding the use of conventional scales, chords and cadences. Instead he wrote melodies that used modes and whole tone scales; his triads were sometimes built on 4ths rather than 3rds (this is called **quartal harmony**), and he would often move 7th and 9th chords up and down in parallel motion. Debussy's orchestral pieces were full of new combinations of instrumental sound and texture, unusual rhythmic groupings and detailed tempo, phrasing and dynamics to achieve the subtle light and shade he wanted. Listen to *L'Apres-midi d'un faune* (1894) or the piano *Preludes* to get a feel for this unique musical style.

Arnold Schoenberg (1874–1951)

As with Monteverdi and Beethoven before, Schoenberg is a composer who stands between two style periods. He began his career as a Romantic composer writing music that was both highly polyphonic and harmonically complex. Schoenberg began to realise that he had reached the end of what he could say within the tonal system, and although other composers were moving towards the same position, he was the first to break ranks and produce the first atonal music. The dissonant sound of this music is challenging to listen to even now, but back in the early 20th century, Schoenberg risked controversy and alienation with this new direction. This new style was called **Expressionism**, because it sought to express darker emotions such as fear.

The first atonal pieces (e.g. *Six Little Pieces* for piano, 1911) were short, sometimes only a few bars long. One of the main problems with discarding the tonal system was that suddenly the means by which longer pieces were structured was gone.

Schoenberg had to develop a new way of organising his music to give it more length and unity, and he devised a system he called the **Twelve-note system**, also known as **Serialism**. The twelve notes of the chromatic scale are first arranged in any order of the composer's choosing (the **prime order** or **tone row**). Melodies and harmonies can be created from the tone row as long as the notes in the row are used in strict order. More variety is achieved through developing the tone row by **transposing** it, or using it in **retrograde** (backwards), **inversion** (upside down) or **retrograde inversion** (a combination of both). Another technique Schoenberg invented was **sprechgesang**, a vocal style combining both singing and speech, which he used in *Pierrot Lunaire* (Moonstruck Pierrot), for soprano accompanied by five instruments. Two of Schoenberg's pupils, Webern and Berg, adopted his methods and the three of them became known collectively as the **Second Viennese School**.

Neo-classicism

Some composers reacted against Romanticism by taking their inspiration from the music of the Baroque and Classical periods, when melody, structure and texture had more clarity. Many older structures and genres were rediscovered, such as concerto grosso and fugue. Neo-classical music can sometimes be hard to distinguish from the older styles it is based upon, because much of the melodic and harmonic language uses tonality. The differences often lie in the instrumentation, some abrupt changes of key, chords often coloured with added notes and dissonances, and a rhythmic approach which belongs more in the 20th century than the 18th. Neo-classical composers include Prokofiev (*Classical Symphony*), Stravinsky (*Pulcinella Suite*, based on music by the Baroque composer Pergolesi) and Shostakovich (*24 Preludes and Fugues* for piano, inspired by those of J. S. Bach).

Minimalism

This is a style based upon very small rhythmic and melodic motifs which are heavily repeated and gradually evolve and develop as the music progresses. Minimalism has its roots in the hypnotic beats of African drumming, with frequent syncopations, polyrhythms (different metres being played simultaneously) and layering of percussive textures. The American composer Steve Reich (born 1936) is the pioneer of Minimal music and he has used many different media to create his music: *Clapping Music*, for two musicians to play anywhere; *Come out*, composed with tape loops; and *New York Counterpoint*, for solo clarinet accompanied by a recorded tape of layered clarinet loops.

Experimental music – the avant-garde

From the 1950s onwards, a number of composers have written music which challenges the very notion of what music is. Using new instruments such as the **Theremin**, the **synthesizer** and recording media, they have pushed the boundaries beyond melody and rhythm to create new music using sound as a raw material to be shaped and sculpted. The pieces were either pre-recorded, multi-tracked so they could be manipulated live with a mixer, or a combination of recordings and parts to be performed alongside. Luciano Berio (*Sequenza III*) and Karlheinz Stockhausen (*Kontakte*) were two of the most important explorers of this new sound-world. John Cage was another notable composer in this field, becoming well-known for the use of **chance elements** in his music; *4'33"* relies completely on sounds and noises happening unpredictably. Cage is also known for the music he wrote for **prepared piano**, where items such as screws and bolts are placed between the wires of a piano to create a keyboard of percussive sounds.

WESTERN JAZZ AND POPULAR MUSIC

Jazz

Key features

- **Swing rhythm** (or shuffle rhythm) was a popular beat. Other rhythmic styles adopted by jazz musicians include Latin rhythms such as **bossa nova** and **samba**.
- **Blue notes** are used in the melody and harmony; the 3rd, 5th and 7th degrees of the scale were flattened for greater expression.
- Many jazz pieces use the **12-bar blues** as both a harmonic and structural element. 12-bar blues used the primary triads in the pattern I–I–I–I–IV–IV–I–I–V–IV–I–I (one chord per bar). For variety some of these chords would be coloured with, for example, a 7th, or replaced with a different chord (a **substitute chord**). It was common to use the 12-bar blues in a **head arrangement** (main theme or 'head' – some **improvised** solos – head again to finish).
- Melodies and solos are developed from small motifs called **riffs**.
- Jazz harmony became increasingly complex as it borrowed chords from the Romantic and Modern composers. A system of notating these chords in shorthand evolved which was not unlike the Baroque figured bass (e.g. $Cm^{7\flat5} = C\text{-}E_\flat\text{-}G_\flat\text{-}B_\flat$).
- Improvisation plays a very important role in jazz. Soloists (or a group of soloists) would base their improvisations on the **blues scale** or a **mode** that fitted with the underlying chord pattern. Musicians such as Louis Armstrong (trumpet), Charlie Parker (alto saxophone), Oscar Peterson (piano) and Buddy Rich (drums) became known for their **virtuoso** improvisations.
- New playing techniques were developed; woodwind and brass players found ways to bend pitches with **fall-offs** and other **portamento** techniques. Brass tone was modified with a variety of **mutes** placed in the bell (e.g. the '**wah-wah**') and players experimented with **growling** into their instruments as they played. Vocalists improvised as well, using nonsense syllables in a style called **scat singing**.

• Jazz ensembles usually contained a group of melodic **front-line** instruments (saxophones, trumpets, trombones) accompanied by a **rhythm section** of piano, guitar, double bass and drums. Earlier groups had clarinet and cornet as front-line instruments, while rhythm sections used banjo and tuba. Most jazz ensembles were fairly small, except for the big bands, who multiplied the front-line instruments for a bigger sound.

Genres, contexts and composers

The first jazz pieces were the piano rags of Scott Joplin, written around the turn of the 19th and 20th centuries. Ragtime referred to the 'ragged', syncopated right-hand part, which was accompanied by a stricter left-hand part, often consisting of alternating octaves and chords in a pattern called **stride bass**. Joplin spent part of his life playing in the bars and brothels of St. Louis and Chicago; this association between jazz ensembles and small, intimate venues has continued throughout its history. The first '**trad**' or **Dixieland** jazz bands appeared in New Orleans and there are some good reasons for this: firstly New Orleans was a port, where many different kinds of music from around the world could be heard. Indeed, most jazz can be said to be a fusion of African rhythm, American gospel and blues, and European harmony. Secondly the instruments used in the first Dixie bands were military instruments surplus to requirements after the American Civil War. Besides playing in small clubs, these bands could also play on the move, most famously in funeral processions. Another Dixieland trademark was the collective improvisation, which often resulted in some rather heterophonic sounding counter-melodies.

As jazz spread across America and into Europe in the 1920s, it became less spontaneous and more organised as arrangers wrote out parts for the bands to play. The ensembles grew into **Big Bands**, with tight ensemble work and virtuoso leaders such as Benny Goodman (clarinet) and Glenn Miller (trombone). This was the era of **Swing**, which lasted through the 1930s and early 1940s, with the Big Bands making records, radio broadcasts and playing in dance halls.

Economic times were hard after World War Two, and jazz bands became smaller again, but their music was faster and more technically demanding with more complex harmonies. This style became known as **Be-bop** and its leading lights were Charlie Parker (alto sax) and Dizzy Gillespie (trumpet). In the 1960s be-bop gave way to **'modern' or 'cool' jazz**, led by Stan Getz (alto sax) and Miles Davis (trumpet). Modern jazz was a logical progression from be-bop with further rises in tempo, technicality, experimentation and harmonic complexity. This marks the point where jazz lost its mass appeal, being replaced by the emergence of rock'n'roll and 'pop' music.

Popular Music

Better known as 'pop', from the 1950s to the present day this has been used as a term to describe non-classical music. Like Western classical music, pop has evolved over time; the main difference is that pop has changed and developed much more quickly through hundreds of new styles and fashions – too numerous for detailed discussion here.

Key features

- Almost all pop music is based around songs with a structure built from sections (**introduction, verse, bridge, chorus, middle eight, instrumental solos, coda**). Bridges and middle eights are sometimes used to bring variety and contrast to the songs.
- Most pop music is in **common time** (4 beats in a bar) with accents on the 2nd and 4th beats (the **backbeat**). However, other time signatures and metres are not entirely forgotten; they sometimes occur as the result of an extended phrase, and in the music of more progressive, experimental bands and artists. **Accents** and **syncopation** are very important rhythmic features in pop music.
- Melodies, riffs and solos are based on the **blues scale** and **modes** (including **pentatonic**, or five-note mode). Performers often decorate their melodies with blue notes, grace notes, pitch-bends and **portamento** (a glide from one note to another).
- Like jazz, the harmonic vocabulary is derived from Western classical music, although most songwriters tend to keep the harmonies fairly simple.
- Although there is no standard line-up for a pop group, many of them feature electric and acoustic guitars, bass guitar, drum kit, keyboards and of course a lead singer. Guitars are often divided into separate **lead** and **rhythm** parts. Many pop styles also call for a **horn section** (typically alto saxophone, trumpet and trombone), percussion and **backing vocals**. It is also possible to hear orchestral and ethnic instruments playing on pop songs.
- New technology has had a big influence on the development of pop music. Musicians have been quick to exploit new sounds from **synthesizers** and **samplers**; **effects** such as **reverb**, **delay** and **distortion**; and recording methods using tape and computer hard drives and software.
- Pop singers tend to use only the 'chest' and 'throat' areas of the voice, because they offer more power. Some singers also use a variety of other

vocal sounds in their music for more expression: shouts, growls, screams and falsetto – a way of reaching higher notes beyond the normal range.

Styles, contexts and composers

Rock'n'roll was the first pop style to emerge in the southern states of the USA in the 1950s. American society at this time was largely conservative in its outlook, and blacks were still being heavily discriminated against by whites. Young artists such as Elvis Presley and Little Richard combined the music they heard around them (white country music and black blues and gospel) and came up with a new style loved by the teenagers, who listened to the radio, watched television and could afford to buy records – but which challenged many long-held values of the older generation. Elvis' rock'n'roll sound, coupled with the new mass media of television, made him a superstar almost overnight.

In the same way that the port of New Orleans was a natural place for jazz to develop, the same is true of Liverpool as a place for John Lennon and Paul McCartney to absorb new influences from America to help them create the early sound of The Beatles. During the 1960s they achieved worldwide acclaim for a series of ground-breaking albums produced by George Martin, who encouraged the band to experiment with different styles and new studio techniques such as multi-track recording, which made it possible to add new parts to those already laid down. Other guitar-based bands such as The Rolling Stones and The Jimi Hendrix Experience achieved similar recognition; Hendrix's innovations in electric guitar technique continue to influence guitarists today.

The late 1960s and 1970s saw new styles emerge. **Reggae** led by Jamaican Bob Marley featured a distinctive off-beat style of rhythm guitar playing called '**skanking**'. Reggae songs were often about political protest, social struggle and the Rastafarian religion. In America the **Soul** sound of Motown Records emerged, a mixture of blues and gospel with a powerful, aggressive style of singing called 'secular testifying'. Soul bands were often larger than the standard 3–5 musicians in a pop band, usually adding a horn section and gospel backing singers. James Brown is regarded as one of the pioneers of Soul and his band were known for their tight sound and choreographed dance moves. Other styles such as Funk and Disco grew out of Soul. New styles of rock appeared: **Progressive Rock**, full of musicianship, experimentation and lengthy songs (Genesis, Pink Floyd); **Punk Rock**, fast, loud distorted guitars, aggressive, full of anger and protest (Sex Pistols, The Clash); **Heavy Metal**, also aggressive with distorted guitars but a more considered approach to song-writing (Led Zeppelin, Black Sabbath). On the pop front the Swedish band Abba achieved global commercial success with effective, catchy songs written by Benny Andersson and Bjorn Ulvaeus.

Hip-hop and rap

Hip-hop started in the Bronx, New York, in the mid-1970s among the young African-American community, and was one of the first pop styles to rely largely on technology rather than live instruments. **Record decks**, **drum machines**, samplers and synthesizers were the main instruments used to provide a looped backing for vocalists who rapped their songs in a mostly spoken style, skilfully using rhythm and phrasing instead of singing. Hip-hop features many distinctive techniques such as **scratching**, a sound effect created by rapidly moving a vinyl record back and forth across the needle of the record deck. Another was **beat boxing**, where the rappers would imitate the sounds and rhythms produced by drum machines and other instruments. **Call and response** chants, which are also found in traditional African music, are also found in several hip-hop songs. Important hip-hop artists include Run–DMC, MC Hammer and Eminem.

WORLD MUSIC

At least one question in Section B will be about music from non-Western cultures, mostly from the continents of Asia, Africa, Central and South America, and Australasia. While this is potentially a vast amount of music to cover, it is possible to give an overview of the music to have come from these places and cultures. You should listen to and learn the key words and instruments for each culture carefully as many of them are unusual and distinctive in both name and sound.

India

The oldest Indian music is known as **Raga** (also called Indian Classical Music) and dates back over 2000 years. It was associated with the Hindu religion and performed at ceremonies as well as for pure entertainment. Raga is also the name given to the scales used to improvise melodies; like Western scales they exist both in ascending and descending forms, but the pitches used in Ragas can be very different. Raga scales were created for certain times of day or seasons; many have been written with for particular moods or occasions (e.g. reflective evenings, bravery or a wedding). Rhythms are based upon patterns known as **Tala**; they often have odd metres and are also used as a basis for improvisation. These two elements are accompanied by a **drone** of 2–3 principal notes from the raga scale. The three typical instruments used in a Raga performance are listed below:

- **Sitar** – a plucked guitar-like instrument, with 7 main strings and several **sympathetic** strings, which vibrate when the main strings are played – this is what gives the sitar its bright, 'twangy' sound. It has a small body and a long neck with frets. The sitar plays and improvises on the Raga scale.
- **Tabla** – a pair of single-headed drums played with the hands and fingers. They play and improvise on the Tala rhythm.
- **Tambura** – a smaller plucked string instrument with 4 strings; it is played in a vertical position. The tambura plays the drone.

A typical Raga performance contains four important structural points, each with its own identifiable musical features:

- **Alap** – the notes of the Raga scale are slowly introduced one by one, with no fixed rhythm or tempo
- **Jor** – a regular pulse is added to the Alap
- **Gat** – the tabla enters, improvising on the Tala rhythm. The sitar improvises on the Raga scale
- **Jhalla** – the tempo increases and the rhythms become more complex to create an exciting finish

Other melodic instruments can be used in place of the sitar: the **sarod** is also a plucked string instrument, but has no frets; the **sarangi** is played with a bow and capable of a wide range of vibrato and sliding effects. The sarangi is also closely associated with Indian vocal music.

Another style of Indian music with both a long history and recent popularity is **Bhangra**, a lively folk dance originating from the Punjab region on the border between India and Pakistan. The main element in Bhangra is the dotted, shuffle-like rhythm of the **dhol**, a large double-headed drum played with wooden sticks. More recently Bhangra has been fused with western hip-hop, achieving wider popularity in the United Kingdom and North America.

China

Traditional Chinese music dates back well over 2,000 years and was used for a variety of purposes, including dance and entertainment at the Imperial Court as well as accompanying Chinese Opera. Most of the melodies are based on the **pentatonic** scale and are either performed solo or in small groups in a **heterophonic** texture (i.e. each performer plays the melody, but with small but noticeable differences). There is sometimes a simple harmony part in parallel 3rds or 4ths. Ensembles are often made up of four sections: a woodwind section with **bamboo flutes**; a bowed string section with, for example, an **erhu** (similar to a violin but with only one string); a plucked string instrument such as the **guzheng** or **pipa**; and a percussion section with drums and the brash-sounding cymbals typical of the region. Songs are usually sung in a thin-sounding voice, often using the falsetto range.

In the years following the Communist Revolution in 1949 marches were written, and often sung with words celebrating the successes of the government.

Japan

There are a number of similarities with Chinese music in terms of when and where it was used, largely because Japan was also ruled for centuries by an

Imperial system. Like China a pentatonic scale was used in traditional melodies, but there are two different versions in Japan, called **yo** and **in**:

- Yo scale – has no semitones (e.g. D–F–G–A–C–(D), or D–E–G–A–B–(D)) and was felt to sound 'bright'
- In scale – includes semitones (e.g. D–E ♭ –G–A–B ♭ –(D)) and sounded 'dark'

Bamboo flutes are also present; in Japan it is called the **shakuhachi** and was played by court and folk musicians, and Buddhist monks played it as part of their meditation. The most important folk music traditions in Japan include:

- **Minyo**, solo songs accompanied by one or two **shamisen**, a plucked string instrument with 3 strings, and a **koto**, a zither-like instrument very similar to the guzheng.
- **Biwa hoshi**, a form of narrative song featuring a solo performer telling epic tales in a part sung–part spoken manner. The performer accompanies him/herself on the biwa, another plucked string instrument resembling a lute, played with a large triangular plectrum.
- **Taiko** – a large, barrel-shaped drum in various sizes played with a pair of thick wooden sticks. They are often played in percussion ensembles whose rhythmic playing is both acrobatic and energetic. Taiko drums were also used in the past to communicate messages on the battlefield.

Indonesia

The many islands of Indonesia are best known for their **Gamelan** orchestras, a centuries-old tradition used to accompany anything from religious ceremonies to plays and puppet dramas. Most of the instruments in Gamelan orchestras are of the tuned percussion variety, and made of metal or wooden bars and played with wooden mallets (indeed, the word 'Gamelan' literally means 'struck by many'):

- **Saron** – one of the smaller 'metallophones'; they play a series of basic repeated melodies
- **Bonang** – slightly larger than the saron, they play an off-beat countermelody that interlocks with the on-beat saron part
- **Gongs** – the largest tuned percussion, they play an important role marking the start and end points of each repetition

Other instruments that can be heard in Gamelan music are bamboo flute, fiddle and voice. The music is directed by a drummer, who plays a double-headed hand drum and signals the tempo changes during a performance.

Gamelan music has a hypnotic sound, with sudden changes in tempo and dynamics. Many pieces use a pentatonic scale called **slendro**; the exact tuning varies from one island to another and is in all cases quite different to the Western pentatonic scale; the closest equivalent Western notes are C–D–F–G–A. Another more chromatic scale known as **pelog** is also regularly used (D–E♭–F–G♯–A–B♭–C), but many ensembles lack the 4th and 7th notes, so there are several pentatonic pelog pieces in which these are omitted.

Latin America

A very diverse range of styles and genres have evolved from the Spanish and Portuguese colonization of Central and South America, but it is also worth noting that the music of Spain and Portugal itself resulted from a mixture of influences from Moorish occupation to French troubadours.

Argentina is best known for the **Tango**, a dance that was once again a fusion of styles introduced into a shipping port, this time Buenos Aires. Tango contains rhythmic and melodic elements from Eastern Europe (polka and mazurka), Spain (flamenco) and Cuba (habanera). The 4/4 metre often has a distinctive off-beat accent after the 4th beat, commonly emphasised by a snare drum roll into the next bar. The other distinctive sound is the melody which is played on the **bandoneon**, a type of concertina controlled by buttons rather than piano keys.

The Andes mountain range covers several South American countries including Bolivia, Columbia, Peru and Chile. **Andean** folk music features indigenous instruments such as the **panpipes**, as well as the imported Spanish guitar.

Panpipes are made from cylindrical reeds arranged in rows and tuned to pentatonic and diatonic scales. Folk melodies are often split between two panpipe players, a technique known as a **hocket**. Hocketing is found in other times and cultures but it is a typical feature of Andean music. Bands consisting of panpipes and drums frequently play at weddings and fiestas.

Brazil is synonymous with the **samba**, a party dance that has almost become a national culture on its own. It is closely associated with the **Carnival** in Rio de Janeiro, during which **samba schools** compete to have the best floats, dancing and music. Beneath the solid up-tempo 2/4 metre, a large group of different percussion instruments (known as the **bateria**) beat out a rhythmic counterpoint of accents and syncopated patterns. The bateria usually consists of a **surdo** (bass drums), **caixa** (snare drums), **cuica** (tom-toms), **tamborims** (similar in size to a tambourine, but it has no jingles), African agogo bells and shakers. In addition some bands have guitars, trumpets and singers.

Music in **Mexico** has a long and diverse history, but of all the genres it is known for, the sound of the **Mariachi** is the most familiar. Mariachi bands typically contain trumpets, violins and three different sizes of guitar; besides the regular guitar there is the larger **guitarron** and the smaller **vihuela**. Sometimes a harp is used, and all of the mariachis are singers. They are usually hired for weddings and other special occasions because most of their traditional songs are about love and romance. In other genres, many Mexican songs have become known around the world (e.g. *La Cucaracha* and more recently *La Bamba*) and the country has produced several internationally renowned artists such as the operatic tenor Placido Domingo and the Latino-rock guitarist Carlos Santana.

The islands of the Caribbean are a perfect example of how different cultural traditions have been fused together to create new styles and genres. Nowhere is this truer than **Cuba**, where European melody and harmony were combined with African percussion and polyrhythm to create many Latin dances:

- **Habanera** – a slow 2/4 style. The main beats are decorated with syncopations, dotted rhythms and triplets. The habanera influenced modern composers such as Ravel, and developed into the tango in Argentina.
- **Salsa** – a fusion of several Cuban dances including **son** and **mambo**, and uses a distinctive syncopated 4/4 rhythm called **son clave**. Salsa has a trademark percussion section of bongos, congas, claves and timbales. Typical salsa bands also feature trumpets, trombones, piano (often played in octaves) and bass guitar.
- **Cha-cha-cha** – a less syncopated dance in 4/4 that took its name from the rhythm made on the dance floor by the dancers!

On the island of **Trinidad** oil drums were recycled into **steel pans** which form an important part of the **Calypso** sound. The top of the oil drum was hammered into several flat spots of various sizes to obtain the notes of the chromatic scale. Steel bands are made up of a 'choir' of pans named after the vocal ranges (soprano, alto, etc.), plus a percussion section. Most calypso melody and harmony is again derived from Europe; melodies are mostly step-wise with a few leaps and chromatic decorations, and the harmony is mostly primary diatonic chords. Although these bands are best known for calypso, they also play a wide variety of other styles, including jazz, popular tunes and even classical music.

Middle East

Although Middle Eastern music covers a vast area from Afghanistan across to Morocco in North Africa, and many local traditions are still continued, the spread of Islam from Saudi Arabia was a strong unifying factor. One of the most familiar sounds of the Islamic world is the call to prayer sung by a **muezzin** five times daily. However, music is also used for dance and entertainment. The melodic scales, similar to those found in Indian music, have up to 24 notes in one octave, which often results in some subtle changes of pitch. Ensembles typically have four players, offering opportunities for improvisation. Middle Eastern music is mostly monophonic in texture, accompanied by simple percussion such as drums and finger cymbals. Rhythm can be complex with odd metres, accents and syncopations, and the patterns are memorised. The best known instrument is the **oud**, a lute-like instrument with 4–6 strings. There are also woodwind instruments; the **ney** is similar to the flute and made from cane, and various oboe-like **double-reed** instruments which sound bright and harsh can also be heard across the region.

Africa

It is usual to divide African music into two main geographical regions, North and sub-Saharan Africa. The music of the North has been influenced by a succession of different civilisations and occupying powers, for example, Ancient Egypt, Greeks and Romans. But it is now most closely related to Middle Eastern culture. Music in sub-Saharan Africa is mostly functional: work songs, music to mark birth, marriage or death, music for spiritual ceremony and ritual and so on. This music is best known for its rhythmic features: odd metres, syncopation, layering of different patterns over each other (**polyrhythm**) are all frequently heard. Ensembles are led by a **Master Drummer**, who sets the tempo and calls the changes in the music. Master Drummers are highly respected within their tribes. There are a vast array of African percussion instruments, drums, bells, xylophones and shakers. The **Djembe** is a single-headed hand drum with a wooden shell; its goblet shape allows it to play a variety of different tones from a high slap to a more resonant bass. Another widely used instrument is the **talking drum**, a double-headed drum with strings connecting the two heads, whose pitch can be precisely altered by squeezing the strings as the drum is played. Many African languages are very melodic and the talking drum is used for communication as well as for music. There are some melodic instruments resembling flutes, trumpets and violins, but it is the voice which is the most important. There is a rich variety of song to be found across the whole area, often sung in a **call and response** texture with simple harmony in 3rds. Other vocal techniques heard are **melisma** and **yodelling**, where the singer rapidly switches between head voice and chest voice.

Europe

There are many forms of folk music across Europe which over time has regularly influenced Western Classical and other traditional music around the world. Most of this music consists of songs and dances as typified by that of the **United Kingdom**. British folk music is modal; melodies tend to have a one octave range and are accompanied by simple diatonic chords. Some instruments have become associated with specific regions of the country: Scottish bagpipes, the Welsh harp and the Irish fiddle and bodhran, a large, shallow drum played with a single double-ended stick. English folk music includes a number of different genres, including Morris dancing, Sea Shanties and the Brass Bands which grew up alongside the Industrial Revolution. In **Spain** the music of the **flamenco** has become known across the world. The main elements of flamenco are the rapid picking and strumming techniques of the guitar, the emotional and high-pitched singing style, and the percussion, much of which is performed by the dancers through stomping, handclapping and/or castanets. In **Eastern Europe** many other dance forms still exist, such as the fast 2/4 **polka** and the more moderate 3/4 **mazurka**.

Australia

The music of the Aboriginal people is among the oldest in the world, and instantly recognisable because of the iconic **didgeridoo**. The didgeridoo is traditionally made from a cylindrical piece of hardwood and produces a drone which can be modified by the performer using vocal and breathing techniques. The drone can be sustained with **circular breathing** for 40–50 minutes without a break. The voice can be used while playing to mimic animal calls such as the **kookaburra** or **dingo**. The didgeridoo is still important in Aboriginal culture and is played for ceremonies, songs and dances. It is often accompanied by **clapsticks**, a pair of wooden sticks hit together like claves. Aboriginal singing is characterised by a complex combination of melodic chants, hisses, shouts, grunts and wails.

Fusion

The IB Music examination often features an extract in which elements from more than one culture can be heard. In the late 20th century, as knowledge and enjoyment of world music has become more widespread, musicians have been influenced by an increasing range of ideas and techniques from other styles and cultures. This has given rise to a large amount of 'fusion music' which is a hybrid of two (or more) distinct styles or cultural traditions. Their sheer diversity makes them hard to categorise, but here are a few notable examples for study and further listening:

- **African Sanctus** – a Mass written by David Fanshawe in the 1970s, which combines a four-part SATB choir with a rock band and recordings of traditional African music made by the composer on a journey up the River Nile.
- **Afro Celt Sound System** – a group formed in the 1990s, they blend electronic dance rhythms with traditional Irish and West African music.
- **Graceland** – an album released by Paul Simon in 1986, which brought a number of Southern African musical traditions to a global audience, and combined them with Western pop and rock.
- **Shang Shang Typhoon** – a Japanese band formed in the 1980s, which blend traditional minyo singing with Western pop, rock and reggae. The band leader, in the true spirit of fusion music, plays what he calls a 'sangen', a banjo fitted with strings from a shamisen.
- **Bhangra** – a fusion of Punjabi music and songs with Western pop, rock and dance elements. Some of Bhangra's best known acts are Golden Star UK, Alaap and Heera.

Sample Questions

The standard wording for Section B questions is 'Analyse, examine and discuss in detail what you hear in this extract.' You may answer these in continuous prose or detailed bullet points and you should allow around 30 minutes to complete each question. Tip: you may find it easier to work out the structure of the extract first as this will help you locate other musical features. Remember that marks are awarded for the following:

- Describing musical elements (instruments/voices, tempo, rhythm, melody, harmony, tonality, texture)
- Using the correct terminology when describing the musical elements
- Outlining the structure of the music
- Outlining the context of the music (period, date, composer, genre, purpose)

Here are the web links for some practice questions for you to try – suggested answers can be found in page 129:

1. https://youtu.be/FWQKSnPrjG4 (0'00"–1'40" score included) Thomas Greaves' *Come Away, Sweet Love*
2. https://youtu.be/T1x2x1nSsE4 (0'00"–1'55" score not included) John Adams' *Short Ride in a Fast Machine*
3. https://youtu.be/89jOPAGJq-M (0'00"–1'47" score not included) Dvořák's *Symphony No. 9 (From the New World) 4th movement*
4. https://youtu.be/cUkHdt2im6M (0'00"–1'42" score included) Mozart's *Piano Sonata No 8 in A Minor 1st movement*
5. https://youtu.be/XpakdPEcyZ8?t=1m22s (1'22"–3'25" score not included) Vivaldi's *Op. 3 no 2 in G minor – L'estro Armonico*
6. https://youtu.be/PvdZ1xIgv08 (0'00"-1'35" score not included) Schubert's *'Du bist die Ruh'*
7. https://youtu.be/_X_1o3Qw4KM (0'00"–1'41" score not included) Fatboy Slim's *Praise You*
8. https://youtu.be/dEWuAcMWDLY (0'00"–1'51" score not included) Aretha Franklin's *(You make me feel like) A Natural Woman*
9. https://youtu.be/oYWC3zQUWio (0'00"–1'46" score not included) Anonymous' *Liwung*
10. https://youtu.be/5-41bBM4lBc (0'00"–1'51" score not included) Totó la Momposina's *Oye Manita*

These web links give away some of the answers for the contextual element of the question, such as the composer or the culture. Therefore, you should try to find some extracts from other sources where you will have to work out these factors from the musical elements you hear.

GLOSSARY

A cappella – literally 'in/of the chapel'. Unaccompanied vocal music, either sacred or secular.

Alberti bass – a type of broken chord accompaniment used frequently, but not exclusively, in Classical period piano pieces.

Anacrusis – a group of unaccented notes prior to the first full bar of a phrase or piece. The equivalent term in pop and jazz is a **pick-up**.

Anapaestic rhythm – in poetry, a word describing two short syllables followed by a longer one. Rhythmically this can be seen, e.g. as 2 semiquavers followed by a quaver.

Answer – in a fugue, the repeat of the subject by a second voice, usually in a new but related key. An exact (but transposed) repeat of the subject is known as a '*real answer*', whereas a modified repeat is a '*tonal answer*'.

Antiphony – a texture in which different groups of musicians have alternating passages.

Aria – a piece for solo voice, usually with accompaniment. Most commonly found in operas, oratorios or cantatas.

Arabesque – in melody, an elaborate florid phrase.

Arco – an instruction to string players to play with their bows, usually after a **pizzicato** passage. *See* **pizzicato**.

Augmentation – a device for developing melodic material in a piece; the lengthening of the rhythmic values of a given phrase or passage of music. *See also* **diminution**.

Augmented 6th – a chromatic chord based on the flattened 6th of the scale, with the outer notes forming the interval of an augmented 6th. E.g. in C major its root would be A♭, plus C, E♭ and F♯. This is known as the German 6th, and there are some variants on this affecting the 5th of the chord; the Italian 6th omits the 5th altogether (i.e. A♭–C–F♯), and the French 6th replaces the 5th with a 4th (i.e. A♭–C–D–F♯).

Auxiliary note – a non-chord note which is a variant of the **passing note**; instead of moving away to another pitch, it returns to the one from which it came, e.g. A–G–A.

Binary form – a musical structure with two distinct sections, which are often repeated (i.e. AABB).

Bitonal(ity) – in modern harmony and/or tonality, where two different chords/keys are heard at the same time.

Blues scale – a scale using blue notes, e.g. C–E♭–F–G♭–G–B♭–C; the blue notes were originally flattened to help create the sad feel of the American blues, but the scale is used widely today in styles and cultures around the world.

Cadence – the final chords or notes at the end of a phrase. The main harmonic cadences are: **Perfect**, V–I (sounds finished); **Imperfect**, 2 chords ending on V (sounds unfinished); **Interrupted**, V–VI/any unexpected chord (avoids a finish by not moving to chord I); **Plagal**, IV–I (sounds finished, the 'Amen' cadence in church music); **Phrygian**, IVb–V (an imperfect cadence for minor keys sometimes found in the Renaissance and Baroque periods).

Cadenza – a brilliant virtuoso passage for a soloist, typically in a concerto.

Call and response – a type of antiphony where phrases from a solo 'caller' alternate with responses from a group of singers/players. Call and response is an important feature of traditional African music.

Canon – a contrapuntal piece or passage where two or more parts have the melody in exact imitation, each entering a few beats after the other.

Chordal – a texture consisting exclusively of chords; they can further be described as sustained, detached or broken chords.

Chromatic – literally 'coloured', a note or chord that does not belong to the prevailing key of the music. It can be used to describe both melody and harmony.

Circle of 5ths – a progression of chords or key changes where each new root or key is a 5th above or below the preceding one.

Coda – the closing passage of a piece, song or movement.

Codetta – the closing passage of a *section* in a larger structure.

Colla parte – 'with the part', an instruction to the orchestra to follow the soloist, e.g. in a concerto.

Coloratura – an elaborate melody, particularly in operatic singing of the 18th and 19th centuries, with runs, wide leaps and trills.

Conjunct – melodic movement up or down by one note; also known as **stepwise movement**.

Consonance – two or more notes that harmonise without tension, a concord.

Contrapuntal – a texture consisting of two or more melodies sounding together. *See* **polyphonic**.

Contrary motion – a texture in which two or more parts move in opposite directions away from/towards each other.

Counter-melody – an extra melody heard in counterpoint against the main melody of the passage. In fugue this is known as a **counter-subject**.

Cross-rhythm – a passage where the rhythm deliberately runs against the main pulse/metre of the piece.

Dactylic rhythm – in poetry, a word describing a long syllable followed by two shorter ones. Rhythmically this can be seen, e.g. as a quaver followed by 2 semiquavers.

Delay – a time-based effect which adds one or more echoes to the part being sung or played.

Development – the middle section of Sonata Form, or any section where thematic material is moulded and shaped through a variety of keys.

Diatonic – a melodic or harmonic passage or piece which uses only the notes of the prevailing key, with no accidentals.

Diminished 7th – a striking chromatic chord built up entirely with minor 3rds, e.g. G#–B–D–F. Notice the outer notes in this example form the interval of the same value.

Diminution – a device for developing melodic material in a piece; the shortening of the rhythmic values of a given phrase or passage of music. *See also* **augmentation**.

Disjunct – the opposite of **conjunct**; melodic movement by leaping to notes more than one step away.

Dissonance – two or more notes that clash, a discord creating tension. Up until 1900 most composers prepared and resolved dissonances, but since then they have been used with ever greater freedom on their own.

Distortion – an effect commonly used on electric guitar, but can also be used on any instrument or voice; it involves deliberately making the sound 'dirty' by overdriving the amplifier's gain control.

Drone – one or two fixed notes heard as a continuous bass, especially on bagpipes. Heard often in folk music and sometimes in Western Classical music.

Drum machine – an electronic instrument used to play and create percussive sounds and rhythm patterns by mechanical or digital means.

Enharmonic change – the changing of the *name* of a given note, but not the actual *pitch*, e.g. C# to D♭. Composers use enharmonic change to effect clever and subtle modulations.

Episode – in fugue, a passage of music used to separate and modulate between entries of the main fugue subject.

Exposition – the first section in a Sonata Form movement, and also the name given to the opening of a **fugue**.

False relation – in harmony, a dissonance where 2 different versions of the same note are heard in close proximity in *different* parts. E.g. a G natural in the soprano heard in the same/similar place as a G♯ in the tenor.

Fantasia – name given to a variety of pieces through Western music history. Generally it refers to a piece in which form is less important compared to those with a more definite structure.

Fugal – a polyphonic texture which uses characteristics found in **fugue**. *See* **fugue**.

Fugue – a **contrapuntal** musical form that begins with a statement of the **subject** (main theme) followed by entries in other parts using the same subject. As the second part states the subject (known as the **answer**), the first moves on to the **counter-subject**, a new theme, in counterpoint with the subject. The opening of a fugue is known as the **exposition**; after each part has made its first entry, the fugue proceeds through further entries in related keys until the tonic is re-established towards the end.

Genre – literally a type of composition, such as the opera, the concerto, etc.

Grace note – a decorative note with no time value of its own (indicated as a small note with a line crossed through the stem) which is 'crushed' in just before the main note it is linked to. Also known as an **acciaccatura**.

Harmonic rhythm – the rate or frequency of chord changes in a passage of music. Harmonic rhythm often speeds up on the approach to a cadence or a modulation.

Heterophonic – a texture in which slightly different versions of the melody are played simultaneously.

Hexatonic – music which uses a scale of 6 notes.

Homophonic – a texture which consists of either a melody and accompaniment, or a passage where the parts move together in the same rhythm (this is also known as a **chordal** or **homorhythmic** texture).

Homorhythmic – a texture in which all the parts move forward using the same rhythm.

Imitation – in texture, the more or less exact copying of a phrase in one part/voice by another. Exact imitation is known as a **canon**.

Inversion – the turning upside-down of a melodic figure, interval, chord or pedal point. If a **triad** has its 3rd or 5th as the bass note, it is said to be inverted.

Lied (plural **Lieder**) – the German word for song, particularly those written for voice and piano during the 19th century to Romantic poems.

L'istesso tempo – play the new section or movement at the same tempo as the last.

Mediant modulation – a change of key where the new key is a 3rd above or below the old, e.g. E major to C major. This is also known as **tertiary modulation**.

Melisma – in vocal music, a passage where several notes are sung to one syllable of the words. *See* **syllabic**.

Metre – the pattern of the beats in a given bar, e.g. 3/4 time is usually arranged as strong–weak–weak triple metre.

Mixer – a device which is used to combine and process signals/sounds from a variety of different sources.

Modal – *see* **modes**.

Modes – in ancient Greece, when the notes of the scale were worked out, the Greeks used them in 7 different ways, all of which can be found on the white notes of the keyboard, each starting on a different note and each with its own characteristic sound. E.g. A–B–C–D–E–F–G–A is Aeolian mode, also known as the natural minor scale; notice that the leading note G is natural and not sharp as it would be in the harmonic minor scale. In tonal music only two 'modes' exist – major and minor, but the Greek modes have had an influence on music across time, place and culture.

Modulation – a technical term used to describe a change of key in a piece of music.

Monophonic – a texture which consists of a solo melodic line with no accompaniment.

Motif – a short melodic fragment which the composer uses to help create a complete theme/melody.

Neapolitan 6th – a chromatic chord using the flattened supertonic (II) triad in first inversion. E.g. in E minor, the supertonic triad is F#–A–C, which is then flattened and inverted to become A–C–F.

Neo-classical – a 20th-century style which drew on the techniques and styles of the Baroque and Classical periods, blending them with modern approaches to elements such as harmony and rhythm.

Oblique motion – a texture with a moving part(s) against a static part(s).

Ostinato – a persistently repeated melody, bass, chord pattern or rhythm; it is often a significant feature of the piece. In pop and jazz this is known as a **riff**.

Parallel motion – a texture where the parts move in a similar direction, but using the same interval between them, e.g. a melody in parallel 3rds or a chain of parallel 7th chords.

Pedal point – ('pedal') a harmonic device where a fixed sustained or repeated note is heard while the chords above it change. Pedals are usually placed in the bass part, but can also appear in the top line (inverted pedal) or in a middle part (inner pedal). Pedals can also be described according to which degree of the scale they are on, most commonly the dominant or the tonic.

Pentatonic – music which uses a scale of 5 notes, commonly found in different cultures around the world. A pentatonic scale can be found by playing on the black notes of a keyboard.

Pick-up – *see* **Anacrusis**.

Pivot chord – in modulation, a chord that belongs to both the old and the new key, enabling a smooth transition.

Pizzicato – (*pizz.*) an instruction to string players to pluck the strings instead of using their bows. *See* **arco**.

Polarised – a texture which features a wide gap between the melodic parts and the bass.

Polychoral – music written for 2 or more groups of performers who are often placed in different parts of the performing space.

Polyphonic – literally 'many tunes'; a texture consisting of two or more melodies sounding together. An alternative term is **contrapuntal**; in the past this referred to instrumental music, and polyphonic to vocal music. Today these terms are used freely to describe all musical genres.

Polyrhythm – different rhythms used simultaneously in different parts.

Question and answer – in melody, a term used to describe a pair of successive phrases which are both similar and different to each other, e.g. their rhythms are similar but each phrase moves in a different direction.

Recapitulation – the final section of the Sonata Form structure. *See* **Sonata Form**.

Reverb – short for 'reverberation', the reflections of sound in a space, e.g. a hall or room. Also a studio effect which places a recorded part in a space which can be specified and shaped.

Riff – *see* **ostinato**.

Ritornello (return) – a musical structure first used in the late Baroque period, which alternates a main section (the ritornello) with a series of episodes, which often use similar musical ideas, a lighter texture, new keys and solo passages.

Rondo form – a musical structure with one principal recurring section, which is alternated with a succession of contrasting episodes. In letter form this is expressed as ABACADA, etc.

Rounded binary form – a musical structure with two distinct sections A and B; however, the B section contains a shortened reminder of A near the end. Not to be confused with **ternary form**, which features a complete reprise of the A section.

Sample – a short digitally recorded musical idea or sound effect frequently used in music production and composition today.

Sampler – an electronic instrument used to digitally record and manipulate **samples**.

Scotch snap – a rhythmic device typically comprising a semiquaver followed by a dotted quaver (i.e. the reverse of the more common dotted quaver–semiquaver figure), giving the rhythm a 'jerky' feel. Popular in Scottish folk music, it is also found in France, where it is known as the *Lombardic rhythm*.

Secondary dominant – a dominant chord which does not belong to the prevailing key of a passage. E.g. in C major the primary dominant chord is G, whereas a D major triad would be called a secondary dominant.

Sequence – the repetition of a musical passage at a higher or lower pitch. Sequences can be used in the development of either melodic or harmonic material, and passages can be described as melodic or harmonic sequences.

Sforzando (*sfz*) – a dynamic marking asking for a note/chord to be played with 'force'. *Sfp* is a sforzando immediately followed by piano (soft).

Similar motion – a texture in which the parts move in the same direction. *See also* **parallel motion**.

Sonata form – tonality-based musical structure often used in the first movement of a sonata, symphony, concerto, etc. First used in the Classical period. The 3 sections typically run as follows: **exposition**, with 2 sets of themes (**subjects**) in 2 related but different keys (e.g. tonic and dominant); **development**, where the themes are explored through a variety of different keys; **recapitulation**, with the 2 sets of themes now presented in the tonic key only. Sonata Form is also used in other movements. Over time Sonata Form has evolved into more complex variants but the three main sections are usually still discernible.

Sotto voce – 'under the voice'. A dramatic lowering of the volume of the voices or instruments, in order to achieve a hushed tone.

Stepwise movement – *see* **conjunct**.

Stretto – in a **polyphonic** or fugal piece, a passage in which the imitating parts are drawn together so that they enter one after the other more closely than before.

Strophic – a musical form in vocal music where each verse of the words is set to the same music, e.g. a hymn.

Subject – the name given to a set of themes in a Sonata Form movement; also the name given to the main theme in a **fugue**.

Suspension – in harmony, a dissonance where a note in a concord is held over into the next chord, creating a brief clash which is then usually resolved downwards by a step to form another concord. These 3 stages are called preparation, suspension and resolution.

Swing rhythm – a jazz rhythm where pairs of quavers are played in an unequal long–short pattern, rather than as two notes of equal length. Also known as the 'shuffle' rhythm.

Syllabic – in vocal music, a passage where each syllable of the words is set to a single note. *See* **melisma**.

Symphony – a sonata for orchestra usually, but not always, cast in 4 movements: fast, slow, dance, fast.

Syncopation – a rhythmic device where the emphasis is on the off-beat notes between the main pulse of the music.

Synthesizer – an electronic instrument which can be used to create and manipulate waveforms and/or samples.

Ternary form – a musical structure with 3 sections; the outer sections are the same or similar, with the middle section acting as a contrast. This form is often expressed in letters as ABA, or ABA[1] if the reprise of A is sufficiently different.

Tertiary modulation – *see* **mediant modulation**.

Tessitura – a term which describes where a musical part sits in the register of the given instrument/voice (high, low or medium).

Texture – a musical element which describes the way in which different parts playing together relate to each other. *See also* **monophonic**, **homophonic**, **polyphonic**, **contrapuntal**, **heterophonic**, **antiphony**, **polarised**.

Theremin – eerie-sounding electronic instrument played by moving the hands around two aerials.

Through-composed – a musical structure which consists of sections each with their own musical material which are not repeated elsewhere, i.e. ABCD, etc.

Tierce de Picardie – a tonic major ending to what is otherwise a minor key piece or passage.

Tremolo (trembling) – the rapid re-iteration of a note/chord. E.g. on a violin this can be done by quickly moving the bow back and forth. Tremolo can be played on other instruments by rapidly alternating 2 notes, e.g. piano or woodwinds.

Triad – a 3-note chord built from 3rds, e.g. C–E–G.

Trill – a melodic decoration consisting of two rapidly alternated stepwise notes.

Tritone – a dissonant interval comprising 3 whole tones (e.g. F–B).

Turn – melodic ornament where a single 'main' note becomes a 4-note figure, literally turning above and below itself by step. E.g. a turn centred on a D would be played as E–D–C–D.

Una corda – also known as the soft pedal and found on the left of the 3 grand piano pedals. When pressed it shifts the whole action to the right so that the hammers strike fewer strings, resulting in a slightly softer and duller tone.

Variation – a musical form in which a theme (either borrowed or specially written) is presented in a series of different musical guises, e.g. with different rhythms or harmonies. This can be represented in letters as A–A[1]–A[2]–A,[3] etc.

Virtuoso – a performer with incredible technical skills.

Whole tone scale – a scale built entirely from whole tones, e.g. C–D–E–F#–G#–A#–C.

SUGGESTED ANSWERS FOR SECTIONS A AND B SAMPLE QUESTIONS

Section A

2018 Prescribed works

The following answer to Question 1 from the *Dances of Galánta* practice questions was written under timed conditions. Even though the candidate has used continuous prose on this occasion, remember that you can write your answer in whatever format you prefer, as long as your content successfully answers the question. Some annotated examiner comments have also been included to give you an idea of what they are looking for when assessing a candidate's work.

Béla Bartók once wrote: 'If I were to name the composer whose works are the most perfect embodiment of the Hungarian spirit, I would answer, Kodály'. Discuss this statement with clear reference to **at least three** passages in *Dances of Galánta*.

Although it was written for a symphony orchestra, Kodály's 'Dances of Galánta' embodies the Hungarian spirit in a number of significant musical ways.[1]

Probably the most important musical aspect was his use of the Gypsy 'verbunkos' dance style, which was used to recruit young men into the Hungarian army in the 18th and 19th centuries. The music was divided into two main sections, slow and fast. The dignified[2] slow dance starting at b50 is played as a clarinet solo, a reminder of the similar single reed instrument[3] found in Gypsy bands. The melody is 16 bars long with regular phrasing, and is borrowed from an original Gypsy dance, although Kodály has changed the original quaver and semiquaver rhythms into something more suitable for the slow verbunkos, with dotted rhythms in every bar, many ending in flamboyant turn-like triplet figures.[4] Another

1 A very brief introduction rephrasing the question. Do not be drawn into writing a long introduction describing Kodály or the origins of the piece – writing about the music is the priority!
2 A well-chosen adjective helps to convey the mood of the music.
3 The candidate has not remembered the exact name of the instrument (the *tárogató*), but would still gain credit for describing it.
4 Excellent knowledge and detailed musical description.

Hungarian feature is that the melody is built from a 2-bar phrase (bb50-51) which is then repeated in a descending sequence. Like many of the Gypsy tunes used in this piece this theme starts in one key and ends in another, in this example E minor, ending in A minor on a Tierce de Picardie (b65).

The second section[5] in a verbunkos dance was always quicker and wilder as can be seen in the Allegro melody (bb236-241). In the tonic key of the piece (A minor), the melody in the violins is an irregular 6-bar phrase, mostly syncopated with a semiquaver flourish in the 6th bar, and is quite repetitive as Kodály goes on to vary and re-score this melody, e.g. b276 in D minor, in parallel 6ths (upper strings and woodwind) and an extension to the semiquaver flourish resulting in a single 3/4 bar among the prevailing 2/4 metre.[6]

A third,[7] even quicker dance is heard from bb443-450. Like the theme at b236 it is built from a 2-bar phrase (bb443-444) – a syncopated falling octave leap followed by descending semiquaver flourishes. In the next bars (bb445-446 1st violin) the leap is the same but the semiquavers stop short on the 2nd beat, and bb447-448 are an exact repeat of the original 2-bar phrase. Finally (bb449-450) the semiquaver flourishes take over and lead upwards into a repeat of the whole 8-bar phrase.

Other Hungarian features include the use of modes, e.g. Dorian on A bb1-5 (the F# is the raised 6th degree in the Dorian scale). Furthermore the return of the slow dance (from b50) at b229-233 is now heard in the Gypsy Dominant scale on B♭, with its distinctive raised 4th (E♮). Some of the other melodies also feature expressive dissonant intervals, e.g. b111 1st violin; the G-F♭, augmented 2nd gives this melody the Hungarian sound of the harmonic minor scale.[8]

In conclusion, Kodály has successfully blended elements of the Hungarian Gypsy verbunkos style with Western symphonic methods to create an art music that truly embodies the Hungarian spirit.[9]

The following answer to Question 4 from the *Brandenburg Concerto No. 2* practice questions was also written under timed conditions. Here the candidate has used a mixture of continuous prose and bullet points. Again, some annotated examiner comments have been included.

Discuss the changing relationship between the solo, ripieno and continuo parts across each of the three movements of *Brandenburg Concerto No. 2*. Refer in detail to specific passages of music.[10]

5 The candidate is using the verbunkos slow/fast sections to not only cover the required 3 passages, but also to continue the main line of argument in their answer.
6 The example illustrating the point is precisely located in the score and clearly explained using the correct terminology.
7 Again, continuing the line of argument.
8 Notice how the candidate uses this paragraph to tie together the other Hungarian features they remembered.
9 A conclusion is not entirely necessary here; this might be better off as part of the introduction.
10 This question is about texture and the different roles played by sections of Bach's orchestra. Be sure to focus on this aspect in your answer; other areas are irrelevant here.

Bach's Brandenburg Concerto No. 2 features 3 instrumental groups; the 4 soloists (tromba, recorder, oboe and violin), ripieno strings and the continuo (cello and harpsichord). These groups are used by Bach in a variety of combinations as the piece progresses.[11]

In the 1st movement the ripieno share in the playing of the main ritornello theme as it returns throughout the movement:[12]

- *bb1-8 – ritornello theme played by soloists and ripieno violins. The cello and violone (an instrument similar to the double bass) have their own semiquaver theme in counterpoint at the same time.*
- *bb15-16 – a brief 2-bar tutti: a motif from the ritornello theme is played by 3 of the soloists and ripieno 1st violins. The semiquaver cello/violone theme is now heard on top in the tromba.*
- *b56 – part of the ritornello theme now played by the cello/violone, while the soloists and upper ripieno strings accompany.*

However, the soloists have their own separate themes which only they play (bb8⁴-11 violin, bb32-35 tromba and oboe in imitation). The soloists also have passages where they are accompanied only by the continuo, allowing the recorder in particular to be heard more clearly, e.g. bb17-18. This is also typical of the contrasting solo and tutti passages heard in a concerto grosso.[13]

The 2nd movement provides a striking contrast to the 1st in that the ripieno and tromba are silent, leaving a 3-part polyphonic texture accompanied by the continuo. This is more a chamber movement than an orchestral one.[14]

The tromba returns to announce the 3rd movement,[15] *and the other soloists gradually enter in a fugal exposition (b7 oboe, b21 violin, b27 recorder), but the ripieno are still silent. At one point the continuo fall silent as well (bb41-46), leaving the soloists briefly as an ensemble in their own right. The ripieno and continuo enter together at b47, but their role here is more to accompany the soloists in detached homophonic chords (bb47-52).*

From here to the end the upper ripieno strings alternate between silence and tutti passages where they accompany the other instruments (b97, simple sustained harmony), so their role is somewhat reduced compared with the 1st movement.[16] *However, the cello and violone do*

11 The candidate briefly clarifies the question and demonstrates good knowledge of the scoring.
12 Remember bullet points are perfectly acceptable in an answer on this paper, and serve here as a good way of organising multiple examples.
13 Good awareness of the significance of the textures used by Bach.
14 There is not much to say here about the 2nd movement, but a brief reference is required by the question.
15 This question lends itself well to a chronological approach when planning an answer. Be on the lookout for opportunities to use this method.
16 Good observation in response to the question!

share melodic material with the soloists, e.g. bb79-85, where they are in imitation with the tromba and recorder. The soloists also accompany occasionally (bb122-125 detached chords for tromba, recorder and oboe) but mostly they are in counterpoint with each other.

Although the relationship between the soloists and the ripieno upper strings[17] does change after the 1st movement, the cello and violone continue to regularly share in the melodic material in counterpoint with the soloists throughout most of the piece. This final point makes Brandenburg Concerto No. 2 a good example of the polarised texture (florid melodies, purposeful bass and harmonic filling from continuo and ripieno) which was such a prominent feature of the Baroque style.[18]

Here is an answer to Question 3 from the Musical Links practice questions again written under timed conditions. Here the candidate has used detailed bullet points based on and developing the outlines given in the tables starting on page 35. You could decide to present your answer as a table, but remember to flesh out the outlines with a more detailed explanation of what is happening in both scores.

Investigate significant musical links between the two prescribed works by comparing and contrasting their use of form and structure.

There are a number of structural links that can be made between Bach's Brandenburg Concerto No. 2 (BC2) and Kodály's Dances of Galánta (DoG):[19]

- *Both works employ a recurring theme, which in Bach's time would been called Ritornello form. A principal ritornello theme would reappear between other episodes of music, often in a shortened form and in different related keys.[20] BC2 1st movement fits this model well, as can be seen below:*
  - *Complete 8-bar ritornello theme in tonic key F major[21] bb0⁴-8*
  - *bb23-28 – now in Dominant key C major and 2 bars shorter*
  - *bb56-59 – now in Subdominant key B♭ major and only 4 bars long*
- *A similar model can also be seen in DoG, with the 1st Dance acting like a ritornello theme, although here the range of tonality is much greater:*
  - *bb50-65 – 16 bars, starting in (dominant) E minor*
  - *bb151-167 – also 16 bars, starting in (tonic) A minor*
  - *bb229-232 – only 4 bars, but now in the more distant Lydian dominant scale on B♭ (with a raised 4th E♮)[22]*

17 Well clarified; there is a distinction to be made between the roles of the upper and lower ripieno strings.
18 Again, good awareness of the significance of the textures used in a wider context.
19 A good time-saving tip is to abbreviate the long titles of both pieces; the candidate has clearly stated their intention to do so in the introduction.
20 A brief description of ritornello is useful here to support the links argument.
21 Remember that many structures are linked to tonality, so it is important to include this information.
22 Good mention of a difference among the similarities.

- *Both works also make use of multiple forms within their overall structure:*
  - *BC2 3rd movement begins with a fugue bb1-46 in F major. Exposition bb1-32, episode bb33-40 and a middle entry bb41-46. This leads straight into a ritornello structure starting at b47 and running to the end with alternate tutti and solo passages in the concerto grosso style.*[23]
  - *DoG has an over-arching Hungarian 'verbunkos' structure (slow bb1-235, fast bb236-607). Within the slow section, there is a fantasia-like introduction bb1-49, and the aforementioned[24] ritornello form from b50. Each of the dances themselves is usually in Binary form AABB, with repeated phrases (e.g. 2nd Dance: A bb96 and 103 flute; B bb109 and 133 clarinet/strings and flute), typical of many folk dances around the world.*[25]
- *Both works use themes or motifs to help unify the piece as a whole:*
  - *BC2: the 2nd movement has a motif F-F-E (bb63³-4¹ violin) which is heard earlier in the 1st movement (bb63⁴-64¹ recorder B♭- B♭- A♭, repeated in a descending sequence)*
  - *DoG: the 1st Dance ritornello theme already mentioned returns much later in the coda near the end (b567). Furthermore, the syncopated[26] falling octave motif used frequently in the 5th Dance b443 onwards was first heard in the poco meno mosso melody at b363 (1st violin). Such motifs were also an important feature of the fast section in a verbunkos dance.*

2019–2021 Prescribed works

Here is another answer which combines prose and bullet points to Question 3 from the *Rhapsody on a Theme of Paganini* chapter. Remember that you can write your answer in whatever format you prefer, as long as your content successfully answers the question. Some annotated examiner comments have also been included to give you an idea of what they are looking for when assessing a candidate's work.

Analyse **three contrasting** passages of music to demonstrate Rachmaninoff's use of variation techniques.[27]

This essay will explore the use of the Paganini theme in 3 different variations. The theme itself is in Binary form AABB, A minor in a fast 2/4 metre. From it Rachmaninoff takes a 5-note motif ACBAE (motif x), a rising 3rd, 3 falling steps and a rising perfect 5th. Motif x is often used when the full theme is absent from a variation.[28]

---

23 A detailed but concise explanation of the chosen example.
24 There is no need to rewrite the example here; simply refer to it in your answer.
25 Good comment, relating the example to a wider context.
26 This could perhaps be notated (♪♩ ♪).
27 Choosing the most suitable variations is key to a good response to this question.
28 Good idea to briefly describe the theme before attempting to explain any changes.

Variation II

- *Still in A minor, 2/4 and AABB form*
- *Piano decorates the theme with grace notes bb1-16, accompanied by a skeletal outline of the harmony (similar to Variation I)*[29]
- *The repeat of B from b17 is different, making this a double variation: theme is played by the flute/clarinet; piano now has a more harmonic role with wide semiquaver RH arpeggios; there are also some falling chromatic quaver triads (b17 upper strings); b21 a B♭ major chord replaces the B diminished chord implied at the same place in the Theme*[30]

Variation X

- *A minor, 4/4 time*
- *Theme is absent, but motif x is present*
- *bb1-8 piano plays the Dies Irae motif in octaves in counterpoint with a chromatic march-like variant of motif x; crescendo into...*
- *bb9-12 tutti **ff** syncopated chordal variant of Dies Irae in alternating 3/4 and 4/4 bars, with a tonic pedal which will continue for the rest of the variation*
- *From b16 Dies Irae is heard in alternate quaver chords split between piano LH/glockenspiel, and upper strings; accompanied by motif x in a running semiquaver counter-melody (piano RH)*
- *b24 the music gradually fades to a quiet end with Dies Irae motif passed down the brass section accompanied by a dissonant falling piano cascade; ends with **pp** reminders of motif x from piano and flute/clarinet*[31]

Variation XVIII

- *The most famous variation, Romantic-style, D♭ major, 3/4*
- *The entire Paganini theme is inverted, e.g. b2³: this means motif x now has a falling 3rd, rising steps and a falling perfect 5th*
- *Piano solo until b13³ when strings in octaves take the melody, piano accompanies with large blocked rising triplet chords*
- *b24³ a louder more emotional repeat begins, but then gradually calms down and falls chromatically back to solo piano again b36; a brief coda follows with reminders of motif x inverted*

Here is an answer in prose to practice Question 4 from the *Surprise Symphony* chapter:

29 Clear, concise writing.
30 Detailed knowledge of the harmony.
31 Good choice of variation with plenty of musical points to mention.

Explain how Haydn's '*Surprise*' Symphony is typical of a work from the Classical period, illustrating your arguments with precisely located examples.[32]

There are many musical features that show the Surprise Symphony to be a work composed in the Classical style popular in the late 18th century.

Firstly there is an emphasis on structure and form. For example, the 1st movement is in Sonata Form,[33] a structure created mostly by Haydn himself. Sonata Form has 3 main sections; Exposition bb18-107, Development bb107-154 and Recapitulation bb154-257. Sonata Form was also based around two contrasting themes (called subjects), which in the Exposition are heard in different but related keys, e.g. 1st subject tonic G major bb18-21 1st violins, 2nd subject dominant D major bb79²-93 1st violins (also joined by flute).[34]

In the Classical period there was also an emphasis on the tonic-dominant relationship, both in melody and harmony. Melodically this can be seen in the 3rd movement Minuet bb0³-8 (violin/flute/bassoon); the key is G major and the melody is built almost entirely from broken chords either in the tonic (bb1-2 and 7–8 G/B/D) or the dominant 7th (bb3-6 D/F#/A/C). Additionally this melody consists of 2 equal 4-bar phrases with the same rhythm, but while the first cadences on the dominant b4¹, the second cadences on the tonic b8¹. This is another typical Classical feature known as question and answer phrasing. Harmonically this tonic-dominant relationship is evident in the regular use of perfect cadences to confirm keys (e.g. 2nd movement bb7-8 V-I in G major, bb23-24 in C major), and also pedals, usually in the bass (3rd movement bb54-62 cellos and basses). Most of the Symphony uses diatonic harmony with chords I and V dominating (3rd movement bb1-8), although there are occasionally some chromatic chords, such as the diminished 7th (2nd movement b142² F#ACE♭) and the augmented 6th (4th movement b171 E♭GB♭C#)[35]

The Symphony is also scored for an orchestra typical of that found in the late 18th century. Besides the strings there were 2 each of flute, oboe, bassoon, horn, trumpet and timpani. Although violins are given most of the melodic material, the woodwind regularly doubled them (e.g. 3rd movement Trio bassoon); trumpets and timpani are often used for suddenly loud, dramatic tutti passages (1st movement b21).[36] The main texture throughout is melody-dominated homophony (e.g. 4th movement), another Classical trait.

---

32 An open-ended question; most features of this piece are Classical style!
33 Careful – very easy to write in too much detail about Sonata Form and ignore other points.
34 Precise locations given here, with bar numbers and instruments.
35 Spelling out the chords gives a clearer explanation of the point.
36 Good summary of Classical instrumentation with examples.

In conclusion, Haydn's use of form, melody, harmony and instrumentation clearly mark the Surprise Symphony out as a Classical-style work.[37]

Here is an answer to Question 2 from the Musical Links practice questions, again written under timed conditions. The candidate has used detailed bullet points based on and developing the outlines given in the tables starting on page 73. You could decide to present your answer as a table, but remember to flesh out the outlines with a more detailed explanation of what is happening in both scores.

In what **musical** ways do the prescribed works both exhibit a lively character and sense of humour?

Both the Surprise Symphony (SS) and the Rhapsody on a Theme of Paganini (RTP)[38] *can be said to have a lively character and some unexpected musical features. Haydn was well known for his musical humour, and Rachmaninoff sought to capture the playful nature of Paganini's Caprice no. 24 in his Rhapsody.*[39]

Tempo – both pieces' lively character can be seen in the frequent use of fast tempi:

- *RTP: Allegro vivace (Introduction); many new variations are marked Piu vivo (slightly faster than before), e.g. Var. IV*
- *SS: 1st movement Vivace assai (very lively); even the once stately Minuet is marked Allegro molto*

Both pieces use syncopated rhythms to add energy to the rhythm:

- *RTP Var. IX piano part is mostly off-beat quaver chords*
- *SS 4th movement 1st subject has a syncopated falling quaver pair motif bb3-4 1st violin*

Sudden dynamic changes:

- *SS 2nd movement has the famous loud chord after the cadence b16; tutti **ff** especially timpani and triple-stopped violins*[40]
- *Haydn uses the same trick again in Var. I but this time puts the loud chord at the start of the phrase (b33)*
- *Sudden **f** tutti passages following a quieter section, e.g. 4th movement b38; also b233 timpani roll suddenly becomes **f** while the other instruments are still **p***
- *RTP uses dynamics in a similar way; Var. XXIII b12 tutti **ff** in orchestra as it forcefully takes over from the **pp** piano passage before*

37 Brief conclusion rounding up the main points.
38 A long title – write in full once, then use an abbreviation to save time.
39 Introduction gives some context to the question.
40 This is the obvious one but there are others!

Tonality

- *SS 1st movement upbeat to b18; music starts in the 'wrong' key A minor before resolving back to tonic G major*
- *RTP Var. XXIII: the reason for the orchestra **ff** mentioned earlier was the argument over the key at this point; the pianist wants A♭ minor, but the accompanying orchestra insist on the tonic A minor. The orchestra wins the argument!*

Section B

1. *Thomas Greaves – Come Away, Sweet Love (score included)*

Musical Features:

Five unaccompanied SSATB choral parts; G major, moderate tempo in 2/2 time; frequent 4–3 suspensions, e.g. 0'10" 2nd soprano and bass; false relation 0'26" (2nd soprano G#, alto G♮); regular cadences, imperfect in A minor 0'25", perfect in G major 0'42"; verses start with homophonic texture, refrains are mostly polyphonic; soprano parts frequently cross throughout; word painting on 'running in and out' (running quaver 3rds and scales in close imitation).

Structure:

2 verses with 'fa-la' refrains;
0'00" Verse 1 and refrain (repeated from 0'12")
0'23" Verse 2 and refrain (both longer than Verse 1, repeated from 0'58")

Context:

English Madrigal, Renaissance late 16th century; modern performance recorded by a chamber choir; originally would have been sung 1 to a part by wealthy educated men and women for social pleasure.

2. *John Adams – Short Ride in a Fast Machine (score not included)*

Musical Features:

Strict allegro pulse maintained by woodblock throughout the extract, but no clear regular metre; clarinets also have a running ostinato rhythm through the 1st section; brass syncopated accented fanfares play in a cross-rhythm to the woodblock pulse, e.g. trumpets from 0'10"; rapid high piccolo flourishes add decoration; brass fanfare idea is built from 2 repeating alternate major chords which change at 0'51"; the harmony gradually changes more often and becomes more dissonant at 1'35"; dynamics gradually become louder up to a *ff* climax with timpani/cymbal rolls at 1'46"; 2nd section starts more softly with a simple ostinato in broken 3rds in lower strings and brass, in a new cross-rhythm against the woodblock.

Structure:

Through-composed using Minimalist techniques of layering and change over time:

0'00" 1st section (woodblock and clarinets)
0'10" trumpet fanfares begin
0'51" a new major chord is heard for the first time
1'09" another new chord with strings and horns taking the fanfare rhythm
1'48" climax of 1st section, 2nd section starts

Context:

A Minimalist style piece for large orchestra to be performed live in a concert hall. Late 20th century (1986).

3. *Dvořák – Symphony No. 9 (From the New World) 4th movement (score not included)*

Musical Features:

Allegro, 4/4, minor key, mostly *f* dynamics, written for large orchestra; 1st theme has clear, regular question (0'15") and answer (0'22") phrasing; 1st theme built from a conjunct rising and falling motif with a range of a minor 3rd, starting and ending on the tonic; accompanied by accented detached chords; harmony mostly diatonic, with occasional chromatic chords, e.g. diminished 7th 1'38"; strings in octaves at start of the introduction; bassoons can be heard playing rising figure near the end 1'46".

Structure:

Opening section of a longer movement;

0'00" Introduction centred on the dominant
0'15" 1st theme has an AABA^2 phrase structure; begins in the trumpets, repeated in octaves, violins play a variant B phrase at 0'42" before returning to A^2 which is extended
1'12" new idea in running triplets, passed between violins and woodwind
1'41" diminuendo into next section

Context:

19th-century Romantic period, the final movement of a symphony in 4 movements for orchestra intended for performance in a concert hall (written in 1893).

4. *Mozart – Piano Sonata No 8 in A Minor 1st movement (score included)*

Musical features:

Allegro maestoso (majestically) in 4/4 time, A minor, modulates to relative major (C); 1st subject features a *f* dotted rhythm motif outlining the falling tonic triad (ECA); contrasted with a *p* quaver rising figure in 3rds with appoggiaturas 0'18", repeated in a descending sequence; 2nd subject has running semiquaver melodies decorated with trills; Ic-V-I cadences confirm keys, e.g. 0'24" A minor, 1'09" C major; melody dominated homophonic texture throughout; Alberti bass accompaniment LH 0'37".

Structure:

Sonata Form exposition:

0'09" 1st subject, A minor
0'25" transition, A minor to unexpected key of C minor
0'49" 2nd subject 1st theme, C major
1'11" 2nd subject 2nd theme, C major; repeated in LH at 1'19"
1'28" codetta, based on dotted rhythm from 1st subject
1'37" repeat of exposition

Context:

Late 18th-century Classical period (1778). This is the first movement of a 3-movement piano sonata intended for performance in a drawing room or small venue, or for private pleasure.

5. *Vivaldi – Op. 3 no 2 in G minor – L'estro Armonico (score not included)*

Musical features:

Minor key, Allegro, 4/4 time; 2 solo violins, string orchestra and harpsichord continuo; main theme features rapid falling and rising scales, and a rising syncopated motif developed as a rising sequence from 1'30"; syncopated motif transfers to cellos from 1'36"; lively semiquaver runs throughout; mostly diatonic harmony with regular cadences, e.g. V-I 1'41"; some chromatic chords, e.g. diminished 7th 2'57"; suspension at 3'10".

Structure:

Ritornello form with alternate tutti and solo passages:

1'24" tutti, main theme
1'42" solo violins in parallel 3rds
1'50" tutti, shorter reprise of main theme
2'02" solo violins in 3rds, then imitation with solo cello from 2'11"
2'26" tutti, main theme in dominant minor
2'43" solo violins in imitation, accompanied by *f* detached chords
3'14" main theme returns, tutti then solo

Context:

A movement from a Baroque concerto grosso, composed for concert performance to an audience made up of aristocracy and wealthy patrons. *L'estro Armonico* was a set of 12 concerti first published in 1711 in Amsterdam.

6. *Schubert – 'Du bist die Ruh' (score not included)*

Musical features:

Slow largo tempo, 3/4 metre, major key, soft *p* dynamic and legato; vocal melodic lines all begin with a motif on one note in a dotted rhythm (♩ ♩. ♪); regular 4-bar phrasing, except for 2-bar extension at the end of the verse 1'02" which has a rising chromatic figure before falling back to the tonic; piano has a broken chordal accompaniment; rubato at the end of most phrases, e.g. 1'04"; diatonic harmony with regular cadences (V-I 0'27") with some diminished 7ths (0'40" and 1'07"); suspensions in the introduction and at 0'43".

Structure:

Strophic song form with solo piano passages:

0'00" piano introduction
0'20" verse 1
1'07" piano interlude
1'21" verse 2

Context:

19th-century Romantic German lied (art song) inspired by the poetry of the time. Popular among the emerging middle class who performed them at small intimate concerts or gatherings.

7. *Fatboy Slim – Praise You (score not included)*

Musical features:

Major key/mode, harmony uses the same triads (♭VII, IV and I) throughout; fixed fast and lively 4/4 metre; syncopated piano chords throughout; lead vocal, electric guitar, bass guitar, drum kit, percussion including tambourine, bongos, cowbell with several layers of different ostinato rhythms; synthesised sounds such as ambient noise (0'00"), vinyl 'crackle' on lead vocal (0'17"), pitched percussion (1'10"); vocal melody range of a perfect 5th, blue notes, e.g. 0'19" and 0'23", ends on tonic, final note/syllable is looped from 0'32"-1'19".

Structure:

Introduction to an electronic dance track built from recorded loops layered together:

0'00" piano and ambient noise
0'17" 1st vocal phrase
0'35" percussion
0'44" bongos
0'52" bass guitar
1'10" breakdown, synthesised percussion and drum fill fades in
1'19" instruments return, along with electric guitar
1'35" 2nd vocal phrase

Context:

Modern, late 20th-century pop (1999), an electronic dance track created in a recording studio for commercial release and for dancing.

8. *Aretha Franklin – (You make me feel like) A Natural Woman (score not included)*

Musical features:

Slow ballad, 3/4 (or slow 6/8) metre with swing rhythms; lead and backing vocals, piano, bass guitar, drum kit, strings, French horns and muted trumpets;

descending harmonic sequence 0'08"-0'18"; chorus melody leaps to a high tessitura before falling back in a pentatonic scale; variety of string textures, e.g. detached chords 0'20", legato chords 0'32", semiquaver fills 0'36"; brass counter-melody 0'47"; bass guitar doubles lead vocal 0'53".

Structure:

0'05" brief introduction
0'08" verse 1, soft dynamic
0'33" bridge, crescendo
0'45" chorus, loud
1'00" verse 2
1'25" bridge
1'36" chorus

Context:

Late-20th-century pop song in the Soul style of the 1960s. Recorded in a studio for commercial release. Aretha Franklin did not write this song, but her inimitable vocals on this recording made it one of her many signature tunes.

9. *Anonymous – Liwung (score not included)*

Musical features:

Gamelan ensemble consisting of a variety of tuned metallophones, gong and hand drum; 4-beat metre; melodic material is in pentatonic mode with some pitches in a non-Western tuning; two melodic ideas – a descending motif 0'07", then disjunct note pairs leaping up to tonic in widening intervals 0'55"; metallophones in groups – one plays on the beat, the other is syncopated, e.g. from 0'55"; the ensemble often slow down together, e.g. 0'18".

Structure:

Organised into regular cycles of 16 beats; the start of each cycle is marked by the gong. The rhythm and texture become busier as the music progresses.

0'00" short introduction, ad lib tempo
0'07" 1st cycle
0'29" 2nd cycle
0'55" 3rd cycle, shorter halved note lengths giving a double time feel
1'21" 4th cycle

Context:

Percussion ensemble found in the islands of Indonesia, especially Java and Bali, played at formal occasions, traditional ceremonies and drama/dance.

10. Totó la Momposina *Oye Manita*

Musical features:

Moderate tempo, mostly in 4/4 but with occasional 2/4 phrase extensions; minor key, harmony centred around V^7 and I; lead vocal, acoustic nylon-stringed guitars strumming chords, brighter sounding steel string guitar soloing between vocal passages, congas played with the hands, handclaps, bass guitar; verse melody has a range of a perfect 5th (tonic to dominant), chorus a wider range of just over an octave; ad lib vocal shouts from 1'11" add energy; conga rhythms keep the pulse and improvise fills.

Structure:

0'00" introduction with a syncopated steel string guitar riff
0'16" 1st verse
0'43" chorus
1'06" interlude; guitar solo
1'41" 2nd verse

Context:

Latin American style song recorded in a studio for commercial release. The simple repetition of the melody and harmony suggests a traditional folk song. Totó la Momposina is a Columbian singer whose songs have been sampled by the likes of Jay Z.

INDEX

bonang 105
bossa nova 97
Brahms, Johannes 91
Brandenburg Concerto No. 2 in F Major
     BWV1047 (c.1719–21) (Bach) 2, 11
  1st movement 12–15
  2nd movement, Andante 15–17
  3rd movement, Allegro assai 18–21
  and *Dances of Galánta*, comparative
     linking 35–39
    sample questions 39
    sample questions, suggested answers
       for 124–25
  instrumentation 11–12
  sample questions 21
  sample questions, suggested answers
     for 122–24
Brass Bands 109
brass section 90
Brazilian music 106–7
bridge 99
British music 109
Brown, James 100
Byrd, William 82

cadences 81, 87, 114
cadenza 114
cadenzas 89
Cage, John 95
caixa 106
call and response texture 101, 109, 114
calypso 107
canon 14, 15, 114, 116
cantatas 85
Caribbean music 107
Carnival, Rio de Janeiro 106
Catholic Council of Trent 82
cha-cha-cha 107
chance elements 95
Chinese music 104
Chopin, Frédéric 91
chordal 114
chords 86
chorus 99
Christian-Ludwig, Margrave of
     Brandenburg-Schwedt 11
chromatic chords 14, 90, 114
chromatic non-functional harmony 29

church music 82
Church of England 82
circle of 5ths 14, 16, 29, 114
circular breathing 109
Clapping Music (Reich) 95
clapsticks 109
The Clash 100
Classical period music (1750–1810)
  genres, contexts and composers 87–89
  key features 86–87
Classical Symphony (Prokofiev) 95
coda 99, 114
codetta 114
colla parte 47, 114
Come out (Reich) 95
common time 99
concertino 11, 86
concerto 85, 87, 88
concerto grosso 11, 85
  concertino 11
  continuo 11
  ripieno 11
conjunct melody 81, 114
consonance 114
context
  Brandenburg Concerto No. 2 in F Major
     BWV1047 (c.1719–21) (Bach)
       12, 15, 18
  definition of 7
continuo 11, 83
contrapuntal texture 114
contrary motion 14, 115
cool jazz 98
Corelli, Arcangelo 11, 84, 85
countermelody 32, 115
counterpoint 13, 14, 21, 32
countersubject 15, 16, 17, 115
Couperin, François 85
Courante 85
crescendo 87
cross-rhythm 56, 115
Cuban music 107
cuica 106

da capo aria 84
dactylic rhythm 12, 115
dance rhythms 92
Dances of Galanta (1993) (Kodály) 23

Lully, Jean-Baptiste 84
lute song (ayre) 82
lyrical melodies 90

madrigals 82
The Magic Flute (Mozart) 89
mambo dance 107
Mariachi 107
Marley, Bob 100
The Marriage of Figaro (Mozart) 89
Martin, George 100
masses 82
Master Drummer 108
mazurka 109
MC Hammer 101
McCartney, Paul 100
mediant modulation 116
melisma 109, 117
melody 86
    *Brandenburg Concerto No. 2 in F Major
        BWV1047* (c.1719–21) (Bach) 13,
        16, 19, 36
    Dances of Galanta (1993) (Kodály) 26, 36
    definition of 6
    Rhapsody on a Theme of Paganini (1934)
        (Rachmaninoff) 53, 74
    Symphony No. 94 in G Major 'Surprise'
        (1791) (Haydn) 61, 64, 67, 69, 74
Mendelssohn, Felix 91
metre 117
Mexican music 107
Middle Eastern music 108
middle eight 99
middle entries 86
'Mighty Handful' 92
Miller, Glenn 98
minimalism 95
Minuet 88
Minyo 105
mixer 117
modern jazz 98
Modern period music
    experimental music (avant-garde) 95
    impressionism 93–94
    key features 93
    minimalism 95
    neo-classicism 94–95
    Arnol Schoenberg 94
modes 81, 97, 99, 117

modulation 117
Monet, Claude 93
monody 83
monophonic texture 117
Monteverdi, Claudio 82, 84, 94
Morley, Thomas 82
Morris dancing 109
motets 82
motifs
    *Brandenburg Concerto No. 2 in F Major
        BWV1047* (c.1719–21) (Bach) 12
    definition of 117
Motown Records 100
*Mozart – Piano Sonata No 8 in A Minor 1st
    movement* 131
Mozart, Wolfgang Amadeus 86, 87, 89
muezzin 108
musical terms and devices 5–7
music-dramas 92
Mussorgsky, Modest 24, 92
mutes 97

Nationalism 92
natural minor 45
Neapolitan 6th 117
neo-classicalism 117
neo-classicism 94–95
New York Counterpoint (Reich) 95
ney 108

oblique motion 117
Octet 89
opera 84, 89
oratorios 85
ornaments 83
ostinato 32, 117
oud 108

Paganini, Niccolò 43, 44, 45
Palestrina, Giovanni Pierluigi da 82
panpipes 106
parallel 4ths and 5ths 30
parallel motion 15, 117
Parker, Charlie 97, 98
passing note 114
pavane 83
pedal points 87, 117
pelog scale 106
pentatonic scale 99, 104, 117